*"For God is a Spirit, and He longs to
have sincere worshipers who adore Him
in the realm of the Spirit and in truth."*
John 4:24 TPT

© 2025 Algorithms of the Living Stones by Bianca van Staden

All rights reserved. No part of this book may be reproduced, distributed or transmitted in any form or by any means, including photocopying, recording or other electronic or mechanical methods, without the prior written permission of the author, except in the case of brief quotations embodied in critical reviews and certain other noncommercial uses permitted by copyright law. For permission requests, please contact the author at oakministriessa@gmail.com.

This work is acknowledged as an original creation by the author. The content of this book is based on the revelation and understanding of the author and is not to be considered religious law.

Bible references used from The NIV Translation, The Amplified Version and The Passion Translation.

Published by Seraph Creative in 2025

United States / United Kingdom / South Africa / Australia

www.seraphcreative.org

All rights reserved. No part of this book, artwork included, may be used or reproduced in any matter without the written permission of the publisher.

ISBN 978-1-964959-34-4

eBook 978-1-964959-35-1

Typesetting/Layout: Seraph Creative

Image Credit:

Cover image - ChatGPT Image Generator, interior images: DALL-E

ALGORITHMS
of the Living Stones

Bianca van Staden

CONTENTS

Introduction — 6

Part 1: Understanding

Chapter 1: The 12 Tribes and the Precious Stones — 10

Chapter 2: Algorithms — 26

Chapter 3: Frequency and Heavenly Technologies — 33

Part 2: Algorithms

Chapter 4: Heavenly Blueprints, Formulas and Angelic Assistance — 44

Chapter 5: Algorithm of Worship and Intercession — 48

Chapter 6: Algorithm of the Trading Floor — 56

Chapter 7: Algorithm of Inheritance — 64

Chapter 8: Algorithm of Immortality — 76

Part 3: Alchemy of Crystals

Chapter 9: Properties of the 12 Precious Stones — 87

Chapter 10: A Guide to Cleansing Gemstones — 126

A Word from the Author — 129

About the Author — 131

About Seraph Creative — 132

INTRODUCTION

In the deep and unexplored territories of the glory realms, exist dimensions beyond our human comprehension where every facet of our being undergo a complete transformation and transfiguration. Invited as explorers of the deep, we are granted the opportunity to uncover the celestial mysteries in these glorious dimensions illuminated by His divine light.

> "Come and be His "living stones" who are continually being assembled into a sanctuary for God. For now you serve as holy priests, offering up spiritual sacrifices that He (Yahweh) readily accepts through Jesus Christ. For it says in Scripture: Look! I lay a cornerstone in Zion, a chosen and priceless stone! And whoever believes in Him will certainly not be disappointed. As believers you know His great worth—indeed, His preciousness is imparted to you." 1 Peter 2:5-7 TPT

LIVING STONE

Living: Chai - חי

Stone: Eben - אֶבֶן

As new creation beings we have been divinely programmed and encoded with heavenly technologies such as the living stones. Yeshua is the chief cornerstone and as an inheritance for us, we have been embedded with 12 precious stones. Not only do we posses them, but we also manifest as living stones. We are in union and fellowship with His divine nature and all that He is now, so are we in the earth.

> "By living in God, love has been brought to its full expression in us so that we may fearlessly face the day of judgment, because all that Jesus now is, so are we in this world." 1 John 4:17 TPT

Each stone carries a certain frequency and energises not only our spirit but also our soul's and body's energy field. For us to utilise these stones to their full potential, Yahweh has designed us with rotation devices to shift these stones into various geometrical patterns. Each pattern contains an algorithm to produce a certain outcome. These geometrical blueprints enable us to raise our conscious awareness and to ascend into higher dimensions. In these higher dimensions, we are infused with the frequency and the Light that radiates in celestial spheres. As we embrace this Light and energy, we become it and the energy now being generated from within us starts pulsating outward, affecting everything around us.

Yahweh has assigned angels and beings to facilitate these algorithmic patterns in our inner man, in order to perform His word and to unlock our new creation capabilities. These algorithms are a sequence of well-defined instructions to be used as directions for performing, processing, reasoning and decision making.

ALGORITHM FOR WORSHIP:

The first mention of the living stones and their sequence can be found in Exodus 28:15-21, where the stones were made part of the high priest's ephod. The ephod was used for intercession, repentance and also worship. It enabled the priest to enter the Holy of Holies. Now, as Kainos beings, we are priests according the order of Melchizedek of which Yeshua is the High Priest and through our unification with Him, the ephod with the stones has been made one with our celestial body (our spirit body that is co-seated with Christ in heavenly places and is beyond earth's boundaries and limitations). Interfacing with this algorithm, or sequence, to which the stones vibrate, causes us to ascend into the inner chamber of Yeshua's heart and draws from us authentic and pure worship.

ALGORITHMS FOR TRADING AND INHERITANCE:

During Israel's time in the desert, Yahweh very specifically mapped out the sequence of how the tribes were to be positioned around the tabernacle. This was a blueprint of a trading floor, signifying each tribe's position of government. Similarly, the tribes were given a divine sequence of how they were to enter Canaan and in which order they were to possess their inheritance. Engaging with our living stones according to these blueprints establish heavenly trading routes between us and the treasuries of heaven. Trading routes are trafficked by angels who impart to us spiritual substance to be made manifest on the earth. Angels of living stones work alongside the angels of prosperity and together their partnership position us in the glorious abundance of Yahweh and creates environments of favour around us.

ALGORITHM FOR IMMORTALITY:

Revelations 21:19-20 reveals to us the detail of the foundation stones in the wall of the new Jerusalem. Before Christ's resurrection the Kingdom was, to man, a destination but as new creation beings, it is now a possession. We are limitless because we ARE the Kingdom of Light. Death and decay have been eternally removed and through activating our living stones and manifesting them, everlasting life starts to pulsate from out of us, redeeming all things and removing death and lack from the earth.

> *"By contrast, we have already come near to God in a totally different realm, the Zion-realm, for we have entered the city of the Living God, which is the New Jerusalem in heaven! We have joined the festal gathering of myriads of angels in their joyous celebration!" Hebrews 12:22 TPT*

PRAYER

Yeshua, like depositing a treasure chest into us, You have given us all things pertaining to life and godliness. As we press in to revelation and understanding, we pray for an interfacing with and a charging of our living stones within our Elohim design. We cause them to vibrate in accordance with their resonant frequencies, to facilitate divine blueprints and algorithms, unlocking our new creation body and manifesting original intent. We partner with Your Spirit and the angelic to lead us into the full truth where knowledge becomes a knowing. Let all of creation declare the goodness of Your Name, Yeshua!

Amen.

CHAPTER 1
The 12 Tribes and the Precious Stones

Gemstones, referred to as precious stones in the Bible, go far beyond mere adornment or material value. These stones carry profound spiritual significance, representing both the tribes of Israel, as the initial representatives of God's government, as well as the divine nature of the redeemed ones as "living stones". These living stones represent a beautiful reality - a divine inheritance given to the sons of Yahweh. To fully grasp their significance, we must look beyond their physical properties and understand their spiritual essence. We will start by laying the foundations.

Living stones in Hebrew is Chai (חי) and Eben (אֶבֶן).

Chai (חי) means "life" or "living" and holds weighty cultural and spiritual significance in ancient Jewish tradition. Through Hebrew numerology (gematria), it equals 18—making this number particularly auspicious and commonly used for gifts and donations. The symbol, often worn as jewellery and used in the toast "L'chaim!" (To life!), represents vitality, blessing, and perseverance. As part of many Hebrew names, blessings, and phrases, Chai embodies the philosophical principle of choosing and celebrating life. Eben (אֶבֶן), the Hebrew word for "stone," also carries deep symbolic meaning beyond its literal definition. While primarily referring to natural stones and building materials, it represents permanence, endurance, strength, and unwavering truth. In mystical interpretations the word can be broken down into "av" (father) and "ben" (son), suggesting connection and continuity, while stones themselves are viewed as vessels of spiritual energy. This rich symbolism bridges both physical and spiritual realms in Jewish culture.

The first Biblical mention of gemstones is recorded in Exodus 28:15-21, where Yahweh instructs Moses on the design and creation of the high priest's breastplate:

> "Fashion a breast piece for making decisions—the work of skilled hands. Make it like the ephod: of gold, and of blue, purple and scarlet yarn, and of finely twisted linen. It is to be square—a span long and a span wide—and folded double. Then mount four rows of precious stones on it. The first row shall be carnelian, chrysolite and beryl; the second row shall be turquoise, lapis lazuli and emerald; the third row shall be jacinth, agate and amethyst; the fourth row shall be topaz, onyx and jasper. Mount them in gold filigree settings.
>
> There are to be twelve stones, one for each of the names of the sons of Israel, each engraved like a seal with the name of one of the twelve tribes." Exodus 28:15-21 NIV

Each of the stones represented one of the twelve tribes of Israel with their names engraved on it. This arrangement symbolised the high priest bearing the names of God's people before the Lord, a powerful image of intercession and representation.

In addition to the breastplate, two onyx stones were placed on the ephod's shoulders, each engraved with six names of the tribes. This placement represents government and is testimony to the prophecy of Yeshua, the Messiah's, reign in Isaiah:

> "For to us a Child shall be born, to us a Son shall be given; And the government shall be upon His shoulder, And His name shall be called Wonderful Counsellor, Mighty God, Everlasting Father, Prince of Peace. There shall be no end to the increase of His government and of peace. He shall rule on the throne of David and over His kingdom, to establish it and to uphold it with justice and righteousness. From that

> *time forward and forevermore. The zeal of the Lord of hosts will accomplish this." Isaiah 9:6-7 AMP*

This parallel proves that, just as the high priest carried the names of the tribes on his shoulders, Christ carries the government of His kingdom. As sons, we are called to share in this responsibility and authority as we are ambassadors of His Kingdom and co-heirs with Yeshua.

In 1 Peter 2:5 He invites us to form part of Zion, His holy mountain:

> *"Come and be His living stones who are continually being assembled into a sanctuary for God. For now you serve as holy priests, offering up spiritual sacrifices that He readily accepts through Jesus Christ." 1 Peter 2:5 TPT*

This verse reveals our true identity in Christ. We are not just followers or servants, but living stones ourselves, integral parts of Yahweh's predestined design. It is our original intent. To be a living stone is to share in the nature of Christ, the ultimate Living- and Corner Stone.

As explained in the beginning of the chapter, 'Living Stone' combines 'Chai' (Life) and 'Eben' (Stone), with 'ben' also meaning 'son'. This linguistic connection underscores an incorruptible truth: our identity as living stones is intrinsically linked to our sonship in Christ. Being a living stone is a derivative of sonship, evidently being grafted from the rock who is Yahweh as He Himself manifests as the living stones. Revelation 4:1-6 describes John's ascension where God's appearance is likened to precious stones:

> *"Then suddenly, after I wrote down these messages, I saw a portal open into the heavenly realm, and the same trumpet-voice I heard speaking with me at the beginning said, "Ascend into this realm! I want to reveal to you what must happen after this." Instantly I was taken into the spirit realm, and behold—I saw a heavenly throne being set in place and someone seated upon it. His appearance was sparkling like crystal and glowing like a carnelian gemstone.*

Surrounding the throne was a circle of green light, like an emerald rainbow. Encircling the great throne were twenty-four thrones with elders in glistening white garments seated upon them, each wearing a golden crown of victory. And pulsing from the throne were blinding flashes of lightning, crashes of thunder, and voices. And burning before the throne were seven blazing torches, which represent the seven Spirits of God. And in front of the throne there was pavement like a crystal sea of glass. Around the throne and on each side stood four living creatures, full of eyes in front and behind." Revelation 4:1-6 TPT

This description reinforces the ecstatic connection between God's divine nature and these precious stones.

As sons of God and co-heirs in Christ, we not only interact with living stones but also manifest as living stones before Yahweh. **This dual nature - possessing and being - speaks to the depths of our spiritual inheritance.** Our invitation to be made manifest as God's precious and living stones ushers us into unexplored territories of the glory realm. Here, we experience a spiritual metamorphosis mirroring Christ's transfiguration. In this realm mysteries are revealed and we remember the truths of the Kingdom.

The 12 precious stones of the Bible are far more than historical artefacts or symbolic elements. They represent our true identity in Christ, our divine inheritance and our potential for spiritual transformation. As living stones, we are called to recognise our value, embrace our purpose and step into the fullness of our original design and identity in Yeshua.

> We are what we possess - we are His living stones, built into a glorious temple.

The pursuit in understanding gemstones and living stones may seem novel or even unsettling to some. However, we are encouraged to trust in the innate wisdom of our spirit and in Yahweh's faithfulness to reveal these truths. As we explore these concepts, may we grow in our understanding of our divine nature and our role in restoring Eden.

It is important that we recognise the weight of our divine inheritance. The precious stones we carry are not simple adornments but godly technology with powerful spiritual qualities; and we are called to embody them. Just as the high priest carried the names of the tribes before God, we carry the nature of Yeshua in this world.

Our identity as living stones is a testament to our union with Christ, the chief Cornerstone. We have been birthed from the very nature and essence of God, now being living representations of His glory and power. As Psalms 18:2 declares:

> "My God, my rock and strength in whom I trust and take refuge; My shield, and the horn of my salvation, my high tower—my stronghold." *Psalms 18:2 AMP*

Let us run with this truth: we are what we possess and we are His living stones built into a glorious temple.

THE 12 TRIBES OF ISRAEL

The 12 tribes, each with their own unique qualities, collectively form the foundation on which the nation of Israel is built and is a blueprint of original design for the sons of God today. In the divine plan, these 12 distinct groups come together to reveal the multifaceted nature of Yahweh.

REUBEN: THE FIRSTBORN

Stone: Odem | Sardius

Reuben (רְאוּבֵן - meaning "behold the divine son") embodies the profound mystery of seeing and being seen in the celestial realms. His name intertwines with the divine attribute of El Roi (the God who sees), manifesting the heavenly principle of divine sight and recognition. Like the all-seeing eye of the Ancient of Days, Reuben's nature flows with the spiritual current of divine perception, seeing beyond the veil of physical reality into the depths of redemptive purpose, as witnessed in his intervention for Joseph's life. The prophetic declaration of him being "unstable as water" reveals the deep mystery of mayim chayim (living waters), reflecting how divine presence moves like streams of heavenly influence, unstoppable and ever-flowing. In the celestial paradox, his very instability mirrors the fluid nature of divine manifestation, showing how the Holy One moves between justice and mercy, strength and tenderness. Though his earthly birthright was transferred, his spiritual essence continues to flow like the upper waters (mayim elyonim) seeking reunion with the lower waters (mayim tachtonim), embodying the constant spiritual tension between heaven and earth. His journey reveals the magnificent mystery of how divine sight (re'iyah) transforms into divine knowing (da'at), manifesting the eternal dance between seeing, knowing, and becoming in the spiritual realms. Even in his failures, Reuben mirrors the divine attribute of restoration, demonstrating how Yahweh transforms human frailty into vessels of heavenly purpose.

SIMEON: ZEALOUS PROTECTORS

Stone: Pit'dah | Chrysolite

Simeon (שִׁמְעוֹן - meaning "one who hears") embodies the celestial mystery of divine attention and response in the upper realms. His nature intertwines with the sacred attribute of El Shama (God who hears), manifesting the heavenly principle of hearing beyond physical sound into the depths of chosek (realm of heavenly mysteries). Like the cosmic ear of Yahweh, the infinite One, Simeon's fierce response to injustice mirrors the divine zeal that moves between the upper and lower worlds when cosmic harmony is breached. The Shechem incident reveals the mystery of how heaven's justice seeks expression through the sons of Yahweh, though often requiring the tempering influence of divine mercy. His name carries the spiritual resonance of Shema - the deep listening which penetrates all worlds and moves the hand of heaven to action. The prophetic dispersion of his tribe among Israel unveils the sacred principle of how divine hearing permeates all spaces, transforming geographical isolation into spiritual integration, much as the divine presence itself fills all worlds while remaining hidden. Through this sacred scattering, Simeon becomes like the divine sparks distributed throughout creation, each fragment carrying the potential for restoration. His journey reveals how heaven's severe judgment can be transformed into channels of blessing, demonstrating the alchemical nature of divine providence in transmuting apparent darkness into vessels of light, embodying the deep mystery of how divine hearing (shemiyah) becomes divine knowing (da'at) in the cosmic dance of creation.

> Reuben's journey reveals the magnificent mystery of how divine sight transforms into divine knowing, manifesting the eternal dance between seeing, knowing, and becoming.

LEVI: PRIESTS

Stone: Emerald

Levi (לֵוִי - meaning "joined" or "attached") embodies the celestial principle of oneness, the sacred cleaving to Ein Sof (the Infinite One). His tribal transformation mirrors the beautiful cosmic dance between severe judgment and loving-kindness, as heaven's warriors became vessels of holy service. Like the divine attribute of kadosh (utterly separate yet intimately near), the Levites manifested the paradox of separation for the purpose of ultimate unity, becoming living channels between the upper and lower worlds. Their holy service in the tabernacle unveiled the deep mystery of how finite vessels can carry infinite light, reflecting the divine principle of holy contraction that allows sacred space for service and connection. The transformation of their zealous fire from the Shechem incident into the holy flame of altar service reveals how heaven refines and elevates human passion into channels of divine blessing. Their geographic dispersal throughout Israel displays the secret of how divine light scatters to illuminate all corners, like the original Light of creation hidden yet present in all things. As bearers of the Ark, they embodied the mystery of lifting up and drawing down, carrying the meeting point between heaven and earth, where transcendent glory touches immanent presence. Their very existence demonstrates the celestial principle of restoration, where apparent separation becomes the very means of ultimate unity, revealing how divine wisdom transforms the sons of God into channels of heavenly connection, embodying the eternal mystery of how multiplicity serves the purpose of ultimate oneness and revealing our true position in Yeshua.

JUDAH (YEHUDAH): THE LION-HEARTED

Stone: Garnet

Judah (יְהוּדָה - meaning "praise") reflects the celestial mystery of divine sacrifice in his willingness to exchange his life for Benjamin's, unveiling the ancient pattern of heavenly redemption. Like the Most High who dwells between the cherubim, Judah's royal lineage reflects the sovereign throne room authority of the Ancient of Days. Just as the divine name reverberates through the heavenly courts (revealed in the root ידה of Judah's name), his tribe became the earthly vessel through which the songs of the heavenly hosts would flow, establishing worship in the holy mountain of Jerusalem. His mantle of leadership mirrors the Great Shepherd of Israel, wielding both the staff of strength and the rod of mercy, as witnessed in his prophetic intercession before Joseph, echoing heaven's pattern of mediation. Jacob's blessing over Judah, that the sceptre of heavenly authority would rest within him until the coming of Yeshua, reveals the eternal covenant-keeping nature of El Elyon. Through this divine channel flowed the royal line of David and ultimately the messianic promise, manifesting the ancient pattern of how heaven's glory descends to establish divine order in earthly realms, fulfilling the deep mystery of "as it is in heaven, so it shall be on earth."

DAN: THE DISCERNING INNOVATOR

Stone: Lapis Lazuli

Dan (דן - meaning "judge") reflects divine attributes through his mystical connection to the Ancient of Days seated upon the throne of justice. Like the Most High's characteristic of executing righteous judgement, Dan's tribe wielded the sword of strategic discernment, establishing heaven's justice through paths mysterious to earthly understanding. His sacred name echoes through the heavenly courts, revealing Yahweh's nature of bringing divine vindication to His covenant people, as prophetically declared in Rachel's utterance at his birth. The prophetic blessing of Dan as a "nachash (serpent) by the path" unveils the deep mystery of how Yahweh works through unexpected vessels, bringing forth justice through hidden channels of divine wisdom. Like the protecting angels who guard the celestial gates, Dan's tribe stood as watchmen at Israel's borders, stewarding the heavenly pattern of divine guardianship. Their positioning at the nation's edges mirrors the sacred role of the cherubim at Eden's gates, serving as both boundary keepers and portals to deeper spiritual realms. Even in Dan's complex spiritual journey through the valley of decision, we witness the unveiling mystery of how the Most High weaves human frailty into His perfect justice, transforming the sons into conduits of divine purpose, much as the heavenly court's judgments flow through seemingly paradoxical paths to establish righteousness and restoration in earthly realms.

NAPHTALI: THE FLEET-FOOTED MESSENGER

Stone: White Onyx

Naphtali (נַפְתָּלִי - meaning "my wrestling" or "my struggle") manifests the sacred attributes of Yahweh who engages in what we often perceive as mysterious spiritual struggle to birth transformation in the earthly realm. Like the swift movements of heavenly hosts (as revealed in Jacob's blessing describing Naphtali as a doe set free), his tribe embodies the divine impartation of words of beauty that flow from the upper chambers of heaven. Their sacred and lush inheritance near the Sea of Galilee mirrors the flowing abundance from Eden's rivers, manifesting Yahweh's nature as the source of all blessing and beauty. Naphtali's name, birthed from Rachel's prophetic wrestling with Leah, unveils the deep mystery of how heaven engages in intimate struggle with the sons to birth divine purpose, echoing the pattern of Jacob's transformation where mortal wrestled with immortal. The tribe's swift response to heaven's call (as witnessed in their alliance with Deborah and Barak) reveals how the Most High's intervention pierces through time at the appointed moment of deliverance. Their dwelling in the mountain heights mirrors the celestial pattern of divine wisdom flowing from the upper realms, while their mastery of both heights and depths reflects how the Yahweh moves freely between the heavenly mountains and earthly valleys, meeting His people in every sphere.

GAD: THE MIGHTY WARRIOR

Stone: Amber

Gad (גָּד - meaning "fortune" or "troop") mirrors divine attributes through his connection to Yahweh Tzevaot's warrior spirit (Commander of Heaven's Armies). Gad's tribe embodied the supernatural prowess of heaven's defenders, reflecting Yahweh's protective mantle over His covenant people. The prophetic blessing "Gad shall press upon their heel" reveals the mystery of God's relentless pursuit of spiritual darkness, while their choosing to dwell beyond the Jordan mirrors the divine pattern of sacrificial guardianship in the heavenly realms. At his birth, Leah proclaimed: "fortune comes!", unveiling God's nature of transforming earthly circumstances through heavenly intervention. Their sacred oath to battle alongside their brothers before claiming their inheritance reflects on the Covenant-Keeper who maintains eternal faithfulness in both heavenly and earthly realms. Like the dual nature of the Most High as both Warrior of Light and Prince of Peace, Gad manifested both the strength of heaven's armies and the nurturing qualities of the Great Shepherd, their territory flowing with provision as a reflection of how Yahweh both wages war and tenderly shepherds His flock. Their divine positioning on Israel's borders mirrors the supernatural hedge of protection that surrounds the people of God, just as the fiery hosts that encamp around those who fear Him.

ASHER: THE BOUNTIFUL PROVIDER

Stone: Agate

Asher (אָשֵׁר - meaning "happy" or "blessed") manifests the celestial attributes of El Shaddai as the wellspring of spiritual abundance and sacred delight. Like the flowing rivers of Eden's pleasures (as prophetically declared in Jacob's blessing "from Asher, his bread shall be rich"), his tribe channels the divine outpouring of heaven's royal delicacies. Their inheritance along the shores of the Great Sea mirrors the endless waves of divine chesed (חסד - lovingkindness) flowing from Yahweh to His children. Asher's name unveils the deep mystery of how divine joy flows from the upper realms as true satisfaction. Their holy calling of providing olive oil for the kings and priests reveals how God offers the pure essence of heaven's anointing to those who minister before Him. The tribe's mastery of refining olive oil mirrors the celestial pattern of how Yahweh transforms the common into the consecrated, pressing earthly substance until it yields heaven's illumination. Their positioning along ancient pathways mirrors how divine blessing flows through heaven's appointed channels, while their reputation for shalom (שלום) reveals the mysterious fullness of divine peace that encompasses every dimension of existence - from the highest heavens to the depths of earth.

ISSACHAR: THE CONTEMPLATIVE SCHOLAR

Stone: Amethyst

Issachar (יִשָּׂשכָר - meaning "divine reward") mirrors the sacred attributes of El De'ot (God of Knowledge) as the wellspring of heavenly wisdom and understanding. Like the Divine Mind that comprehends all times and seasons, Issachar was granted the mystical ability to understand times and seasons, reflecting the deep discernment flowing from the upper realms. Their sacred calling as bearers of Torah's burden mirrors how God Himself bears the weight of all creation while sustaining the cosmic order. The tribe's devotion to the Torah study unveils their connection to the Ancient of Days as the source of all wisdom. Issachar's dwelling in the fertile valley of Canaan reveals the divine pattern of how heaven plants wisdom in the sons to bring forth spiritual fruit. The prophetic metaphor of "strong-boned donkey" in Jacob's blessing unveils the mystery of how divine strength manifests through humble service, reflecting the Holy One's nature of bearing creation's burdens through steadfast love (chesed). Their role as counsellors to the tribes mirrors how the Ruach HaKodesh guides from the heavenly council, while their divine contentment to "bend their shoulders to bear" reveals the celestial pattern of finding highest joy in lowest service, establishing divine harmony through willing sacrifice.

ZEBULUN: THE PROSPEROUS MERCHANT

Stone: Beryl

Zebulun (זְבוּלוּן - meaning "celestial dwelling place") manifests the sacred attributes of Yahweh who bridges the divide between heavenly and earthly realms. Like the divine nature of dwelling amidst His people, Zebulun's positioning between the Great Sea and the Promised Land reflects the Holy One's accessibility and ability to connect diverse spheres of existence. Their sacred role in maritime commerce mirrors how Yahweh creates pathways for heaven's blessings and sustenance to flow between peoples and nations. Jacob's prophetic blessing that "Zebulun shall dwell at the haven of the sea" unveils the mystery of how the Almighty fashions sacred refuges and sanctuaries within the ebb and flow of earthly circumstance. Their divinely appointed partnership with Issachar, supporting their study of Torah through their commercial ventures, reflects the celestial pattern of how the Most High sustains spiritual pursuits through material provision. The tribe's mastery of navigating both the depths of the sea and the heights of the land reveals the profound omnipresence of Yahweh, who moves freely between the heavenly realms and earthly domains. Their expertise in commerce mirrors the Divine Provider who establishes networks of blessing, while their courageous voyages upon treacherous waters reflect the adventurous nature of the Heavenly King in pursuing intimate relationship with His creation. Even the geographic positioning of their inheritance embodies the sacred role of Zebulun as a bridge, connecting diverse peoples and cultures according to the eternal designs of the Almighty.

JOSEPH: THE FRUITFUL DREAMER

Stone: Sardonyx

Joseph (יוֹסֵף - meaning "he who adds") profoundly mirrors the divine attributes through his epic journey from the depths of suffering to the heights of sovereignty, unveiling the redemptive nature of El Elyon and His ability to transfigure evil into good. Like the prophetic and revelatory essence of Yeshua, Joseph was endowed with the heavenly gift of understanding dreams and visions, piercing the veil of present circumstances to discern the eternal purposes of the Almighty. His extraordinary forgiveness towards his brothers reflects the merciful nature of Yahweh, demonstrating the divine quality of transforming judgment into redemption. Joseph's administrative wisdom in Egypt is evidence of the sustaining providence of the Most High, while his preservation of life during times of famine unveils the saving power that flows from the heavenly realms. His unyielding resistance to the temptation of Potiphar's wife reflects the unbending righteousness and kadosh (קדוש - holiness) of El Shaddai. Joseph's elevation from the dungeon to the palace mirrors how the Heavenly King uplifts the humble and orchestrates divine reversals within the tapestry of earthly events. His famous declaration that what was meant for evil God intended for good, perfectly reflects the sovereign nature of Yahweh in weaving all things together for His eternal purpose. As the "fruitful vine" (as described in Jacob's blessing), Joseph mirrors the abundant nature of the Divine Provider, who brings forth life even in the midst of barren circumstances. Through his profound journey from suffering to glory, Joseph became the clearest Old Testament prefiguration of Messiah, reflecting how God works through apparent defeat to ultimately bring about the victory of redemption and salvation for all creation.

BENJAMIN: THE FIERCE PROTECTOR

Stone: Jasper

Benjamin (בִּנְיָמִין - meaning "son of the right hand" and "son of strength") embodies the divine attributes through his mystical connection to the dual nature of the Almighty as both Warrior and Beloved. Like Yahweh's infinite capacity for both power and tenderness, Benjamin is described in Jacob's blessing as a "ravenous wolf" and in Moses' benediction as the "loved one of Adonai", reflecting how God encompasses both fierce justice and gentle compassion. The transformation of his birth name "Ben-Oni" (בֶּן אוֹנִי - son of my sorrow) to Benjamin mirrors the divine pattern of transfiguring pain into strength and sorrow into glory. The tribe's renown for skilled left-handed warriors unveils the celestial mystery of how God employs unexpected methods to achieve ultimate victory. Benjamin's unique position as the only son born within the borders of the Promised Land mirrors God's nature as the true and eternal Inhabitant of sacred geography. Their territorial inheritance encompassing Jerusalem reflects the divine presence as the center of all worship and heavenly revelation. As the youngest and most protected son, Benjamin symbolises the Heavenly Father's special care for the vulnerable, while the tribe's zealous defence of their own (even during the tragic episode at Giv'ah) mirrors the passionate nature of Yahweh in safeguarding His covenantal people. The profound transformation of Benjamin's tribal identity from fierce warriors to guardians of the temple unveils the celestial mystery of how Yahweh brings forth holiness from the crucible of human nature.

As these 12 tribes come together, they form a tapestry of diverse strengths, characteristics, and contributions. Each tribe is a unique reflection of the Kingdom of Light, a multifaceted gem in the crown of the sons of God. Through their unity and cooperation, the tribes fulfil the vision of the Almighty, bringing forth a people who are a light unto the nations and a testament to the glory of the One who called them into existence. The tribes and their resonance with precious stones forms a rich tapestry of a divine blueprint for our identity as Kainos (new creation) beings, as well as our purpose as the sons of God. Each tribe and stone, with its unique characteristics and spiritual resonances, reflects an aspect of the original design for humanity and creation, guiding us back to our primordial nature and destiny.

Just as the high priest's ephod bore the twelve precious stones, each representing one of the tribes, so too are we fashioned as living stones, collectively forming the Kingdom of God. Each stone is a facet of the divine, a unique expression of the Almighty's multifaceted nature. When viewed through the lens of sonship, the stones become a mirror, reflecting the blueprint of our original design. Just as these tribes were called to collectively represent the nation of Israel, we too are commissioned to embody the diverse yet complementary aspects of our divine inheritance. We are not passive recipients of God's grace, but active participants in the unfolding of His eternal purpose.

The 12 stones serve as a roadmap, guiding us back to the intentions that were etched into the heart of the Creator before the foundations of the earth. As we embrace our identity as living stones, we recognise that we are not just encoded with the characteristics of the tribes but, far greater, that we are called to become the living embodiment of these qualities and that we have remarkable resources available to perfect His nature in our consciousness. Our task is to cultivate within ourselves heavenly virtues and beyond human characteristics, allowing the fullness of His ecstatic plan to be expressed through us. In the unfolding of God's plan, the 12 stones point us towards the culmination of all things, when the brokenness of this world will be healed and the original blueprint for humanity will be fully realised. This means we become active participants in the restoration of all creation, ushering in the day when the "knowledge of the glory of the Lord will cover the earth as the waters cover the sea" (Habakkuk 2:14).

May we rise as living stones until the day when the fullness of our sonship is revealed, and the world stands in awe of the glory of the Lord.

CHAPTER 2

Algorithms

FROM EARTHLY CALCULATIONS TO COSMIC CONNECTIONS

Algorithms are fundamental sequences of instruction designed to solve problems or perform specific tasks. Their applications span a vast spectrum, from the mundane to the metaphysical, mirroring the intricate connections between the earthly and the spiritual realms.

In laymen's terms, an algorithm is a precise, step-by-step set of rules that guides a process from input to output, ensuring consistent results when followed correctly.

In the field of mathematics and computer science, algorithms form the bedrock of computational processes. They range from simple procedures, like following a cooking recipe, to complex computational methods powering advanced software systems. If man and earth are so reliant on the application of algorithms, where do we think the blueprint for it came from? Any technological blueprint, whether promoted by a son of God or an unbeliever, are downloaded from the spiritual realms. Algorithms essentially mirror divine instructions of creation, biology and the cosmic order. Since Yahweh is the divine orchestrator and master mind of the universe and all its perfect functioning and since ALL things are held together by and in Yeshua according to Colossians 1:17, we can be convinced of nothing other than the fact that the concept of technology and supernatural intelligence comes from God. Should man be responsible for how we steward said intelligences? Most definitely yes! But the praise for ultra-dimensional intelligence and technology can only be accredited to the great I Am. He is the source of all that is powerful and transformational.

Excitingly, the concept of encoded instructions guiding both earthly and heavenly realms finds a parallel in how we understand the functioning of heavenly technologies and resources offered to us to excel in the invitation to co-reign with Christ.

Each of the 12 tribes, associated with a specific precious stone, was programmed with an algorithm to facilitate divine consultations. The stones were by no means decorative but their programmed information and resonant frequencies facilitated heavenly technologies for each tribe. This theory proves a quantum connection between the physical stones and metaphysical realms, much like how algorithms connect abstract instructions to tangible outcomes in computing.

Taking it one step further with this perspective in mind, each tribe was not only allocated a specific earthly inheritance (land) to govern over but also held a seat of governance in heavenly places, reflected in each tribe's appointed gate in the "Mazzaroth" or cosmos. This cosmic allocation mirrors the way algorithms are used to organise and structure energetic spaces, assigning specific functions or access points within complex systems and essentially manifests the connection between spiritual realms and earthly domain.

The stones representing each tribe are believed to have a quantum connection to their corresponding cosmic gate, creating a bridge between the physical and celestial realms. This notion of encoded stones linking to cosmic gates resonates with how algorithms serve as bridges between human intent and spiritual

> Algorithms embody the idea that complex systems, be they computational or cosmic, operate on sets of instructions that bring order to chaos and purpose to process.

Chapter 2 - Algorithms | 27

or energetic action. In this spiritual framework, the tribes were predestined to rule and reign alongside Christ, their cosmic gates serving as points of authority and influence in the universal order. The concept of predetermined cosmic roles parallels how algorithms are designed with specific purposes in mind, each fulfilling its role within larger systems.

Whilst these spiritual concepts diverge from mainstream scientific understanding, they offer an intriguing spiritual lens through which to view the role of algorithms. Just as the tribes and their stones were believed to be part of a grand cosmic design, algorithms form part of the intricate tapestry of merging information and actualisation.

ALGORITHMIC CODES IN THE HUMAN BODY

Within each human body lies a masterpiece of algorithmic artistry, where mathematics and biology dance in perfect harmony to create the symphony of life itself. Our hearts conduct their eternal orchestra through exquisitely timed recursions, each chamber performing its role in a four-part harmony of perfectly optimised pumping sequences. The neural networks that weave through our being create patterns more intricate than the finest lace, firing in cascading arrays of binary elegance that transform simple electrical impulses into the very essence of thought and feeling. Deep in our marrow, stem cells execute their branching logic with flawless precision, following decision trees that would make any programmer weep with appreciation for their elegant simplicity and profound complexity.

Our immune system stands as perhaps the most beautiful algorithm of all – a self-improving, self-adjusting masterwork of pattern recognition that learns and adapts with a grace that our finest artificial systems can only dream of emulating. Each antibody is a living query, searching through the body's vast database with a precision that makes modern search algorithms seem crude by comparison.

The genetic code itself reads like poetry written in base pairs, each sequence a verse in the grand story of the ages and generations recorded therein, running parallel processes with an efficiency that would humble our most advanced computers. Even in sleep, our bodies run their maintenance algorithms with such sophisticated scheduling that they make our best optimisation algorithms look primitive in comparison.

In every cell, in every process, we see the pure mathematical beauty of life expressing itself through loops, conditionals and sequences that have been fearfully and wonderfully created in perfection. We are not merely biological machines running code – we are living proof that algorithms can achieve a state of sublime beauty.

Even more fascinating, the fascial network of the human body reveals an extraordinary crystalline architecture that operates much like a living fibre optic system. Within the fascia – the web-like connective tissue that surrounds every muscle, bone, and organ – lies an intricate network of crystalline structures, particularly along neural pathways. These biological crystals, primarily composed of piezoelectric collagen and structured water molecules, form a sophisticated communication network that some researchers have likened to a liquid crystal matrix.

Along facial nerve pathways, these crystalline structures arrange themselves in remarkably ordered patterns, creating what could be described as microscopic semiconductor pathways. The collagen fibres, which form triple-helix structures, demonstrate properties similar to liquid crystals, allowing them to:

- Conduct bioelectrical signals with remarkable efficiency
- Store and transmit information through conformational changes
- Respond to mechanical pressure by generating electrical signals (piezoelectric effect)
- Create coherent energy fields that may facilitate cellular communication

The facial nerve's crystalline matrix appears to function as both an information superhighway and an energy transducer.

Intriguingly, these crystalline structures seem to exhibit semiconductor properties, suggesting they might process information in ways similar to modern computer chips, creating a kind of biological microprocessor network throughout the fascia. This could help explain the body's remarkable ability to coordinate complex responses and maintain homeostasis through what appears to be a crystalline-mediated communication system.

THE ALGORITHMIC BRIDGE: BODY, SPIRIT, AND CRYSTAL RESONANCE

Just as our physical form operates on precise biological algorithms, the interaction between human consciousness and crystalline structures suggests a deeper pattern of energetic algorithms – where gemstones serve as natural processors bridging the material and spiritual realms.

THE CRYSTALLINE INTERFACE

Each precious stone possesses an ordered molecular lattice, creating consistent vibrational frequencies that can interact with our body's own algorithmic processes:

- Amethyst's hexagonal crystal system resonates with the pineal gland's natural frequency, potentially enhancing its role in processing spiritual information through what we might call "consciousness"

- Clear Quartz functions like a programmable crystal computer, its silicon dioxide structure capable of receiving, storing, and amplifying spiritual data through its precise geometric arrangements

- Lapis Lazuli's complex mineral matrix operates as a spiritual debugging tool, its frequencies helping to identify and clear blockages in our bioelectric field (arche).

THE BODY'S SPIRITUAL PROCESSING

Our biological systems appear to interact with these crystalline frequencies through specific pathways:

1. Our human organs function as a series of energetic processors, each operating at distinct frequencies that correspond to different crystal resonances

2. The meridian network serves as spiritual data pathways, carrying crystalline frequencies throughout the body's bioelectric field

3. The pineal gland acts as a central spiritual processing unit, translating crystalline vibrations into biochemical responses

THE INTEGRATION ALGORITHM

The interactions suggest our bodies possess natural spiritual computing capabilities, with crystals serving as external processors that expand our capacity for divine connection. The geometric perfection of crystalline structures creates reliable interfaces between physical and spiritual operating systems, allowing for consistent and reproducible spiritual algorithms.

Our bodies appear to use the ordered atomic structures of crystals to process spiritual information. This creates a beautiful synthesis where the mathematical precision of both our internal biological algorithms and the crystal's molecular geometry work together to facilitate transcendent experiences.

In conclusion, algorithms, whether viewed through a purely mathematical lens or a metaphysical one, represent a fundamental organising principle. They embody the idea that complex systems, be they computational, biological or cosmic, operate on sets of instructions that bring order to chaos and purpose to process. As we continue to advance in our understanding of both the celestial and physical universes, the parallels between ancient spiritual concepts and modern computational theories offer fascinating food for thought, inviting us to consider the hidden connections that may exist between the seen and unseen realms of our existence.

All things considered, it is clear that even the living letters, by which Yahweh formed the worlds, adhere to a certain code and inherent function. God spoke and the combination of His life-giving breath and sound gave substance to all that was created. The same formula was given to Adam when he was to name the animals and give purpose to creation. It is in our stewardship as sons of God that we tap into this code to have legislative and governmental say in what happens on the earth. Grabbing hold of the living stones as resources gives us great comprehension and understanding which facilitates our partnership with Yeshua's restorative agenda. Yeshua has lavished on us every spiritual blessing so that we can walk in the fullness of His government and Kingship as kings, priests and prophets; and even weightier than that, SONS of Yahweh. We are co-heirs with Christ and all that we do is for His reward. Embracing and utilising heavenly algorithms give us access to the creation chambers of heaven and affects everything under our stewardship and in our sphere of influence.

CHAPTER 3
Frequency and Heavenly Technologies

THE DIVINE SYMPHONY: FREQUENCY, QUANTUM FIELDS, AND THE SPIRITUAL ESSENCE OF GEMSTONES

Frequency is a fundamental concept in physics that plays a crucial role in our understanding of the natural world woven into the supernatural. From the light we see to the sounds we hear, frequency underlies many of the phenomena we experience daily. In the grand tapestry of creation, frequency stands as a fundamental thread woven by Yahweh's hand to connect all aspects of existence. From the tiniest subatomic particles to the vast expanse of the cosmos, frequency manifests as a universal language, speaking of the Creator's infinite wisdom and the interconnectedness of all things. As we delve into the nature of frequency, quantum fields and the heavenly technology encoded in gemstones, we are taken on a journey that bridges the physical and the metaphysical, the energetic and the spiritual and the seen and the unseen.

In this exploration, we will uncover the divine orchestration behind the concept of frequency, its manifestation in the quantum realm, and how precious stones serve as conduits of energies, influencing our earthly atmosphere as well as our physical and spiritual bodies. Through this lens, we see that Yahweh, as the Author of frequency and the Architect of the quantum field, imbued creation with a vibrational essence that resonates with His divine nature.

RESONANCE AND NATURAL FREQUENCY

We interface with a vast array of frequencies daily due to everything being energy, hence why so many things in this natural world affect us in our physical, emotional and spiritual state. **Resonance occurs when a system is able to store and easily transfer energy between different forms.** Every object has a natural frequency at which it vibrates when struck or disturbed. When an external force applies a frequency matching the object's natural frequency, resonance occurs, potentially amplifying the vibration. This supports the idea that the vibration of certain gemstones can cause a similar vibration in the human body or surrounding area. Some studies suggest that gemstones create or influence subtle energy fields that carry information and are able to transfer their vibrational energy to a person or space. Now, as fascinating as that sounds, this knowledge also comes with a great measure of responsibility.

THE DIVINE NATURE OF FREQUENCY

At its core, frequency is the pulse of creation, the cosmic heartbeat that echoes the rhythm of primordial thought. In the physical realm, frequency is defined as the number of occurrences of a repeating event per unit of time. However, from a spiritual perspective, frequency transcends mere mathematical description. It is the very essence of movement, change, and life itself – it is sound and light - a manifestation of God's ongoing creative process.

> *"When the morning stars sang together, and all the sons of God shouted for joy." Job 38:7 NIV*

This poetic scripture hints at the celestial harmony, a cosmic frequency that resonates throughout creation.

THE WORD AS FREQUENCY

The Gospel of John opens with,

> "In the beginning the Living Expression was already there. And the Living Expression was with God, yet fully God. And through His creative inspiration this Living Expression made all things, for nothing has existence apart from Him!" John 1:1, 3 TPT

This scripture can be understood as the primordial frequency from which all of creation emanates. It supports the revelation that the words or sounds (the living letters) that came from the mouth of Yahweh was the origin of creation. It was the intention and expressive energy of Yahweh that created. To quote my husband, Scharl, "God spoke and the living letters that came from Himself, formed words and the words formed worlds". God spoke the words "Let there be light!" and there was light. It was the frequency of His sound that collapsed the sound and light waves to form matter. Is it not also true that Yeshua is the Word made flesh? He is the sound of who God is that became man and realigned humanity into the primordial truth. This viewpoint should draw us into the mysteries of the beauty of the Trinity! His Words should become flesh to us. It should be our natural instead of the supernatural. When He becomes flesh to us through His Living Expression, it transfigures us into our eternal and incorruptible state. That is the power of frequency when combined with glory.

FREQUENCY AS HEAVENLY COMMUNICATION

Frequency serves as a medium of heavenly communication - a way for Yahweh to interact with creation, apart from just our connected awareness. For the purpose of clarity, a medium is defined as the substance that transfers energy or light from one substance, place or surface to another. The medium acts as a carrier that can transfer any form of energy, sound wave, light or heat.

> His Word should become flesh to us. It should be our natural instead of the supernatural.

As sons of God and Kainos (new creation) beings, we are tethered to the heart of Yeshua and therefore tethered to the throne and mercy seat of our Father. This union establishes an open communication line between our spirit and the Holy Spirit. Our spirit, who is seated in heavenly places alongside Yeshua, became the medium through which Holy Spirit can transfer information from the spiritual realms to our soul. But in the Bible, we find numerous instances of God communicating not through His Holy Spirit but through sound or vibration. The voice of God speaking to Moses from the burning bush (fire being the medium), the trumpet blasts at Mount Sinai (sound being the medium) and the still small voice heard by Elijah (wind being the medium) all point to different manifestations of His divine frequency being perceived by man.

FREQUENCY IN THE QUANTUM FIELD

The Quantum Symphony

As we aim to understand frequency and energy and how it affects our physical and spiritual realities, we need to have a brief understanding of the fascinating world of quantum physics. Here, at the most fundamental level of existence, we find a realm that seems to echo spiritual truths long held by mystics and sages. The quantum field, a concept in modern physics, can be viewed as the canvas upon which God paints the masterpiece of creation. In quantum field theory particles are understood not as discrete entities but as excitations or vibrations in underlying (quantum or spiritual) fields. These vibrations, or frequencies, determine the nature and properties of particles. From this perspective, the entire universe can be seen as a vast, interconnected web of vibrational fields – a quantum symphony orchestrated by the Divine Conductor.

Two key concepts in quantum mechanics – superposition and entanglement – offer profound spiritual insights.

Superposition, the idea that a particle can exist in multiple states simultaneously until observed, mirrors the spiritual concept of divine omnipresence. Just as God is understood to be everywhere at once, quantum particles exhibit a similar transcendence of ordinary spatial limitations.

Quantum entanglement, where particles become interconnected in such a way that the quantum state of each particle cannot be described independently, even when separated by large distances, speaks to the fundamental unity of creation and heavenly dimensions. This phenomenon, which Einstein famously referred to as "spooky action at a distance," aligns with our belief about the interconnectedness of all things in God's creation.

THE OBSERVER EFFECT AND DIVINE CONSCIOUSNESS

The observer effect in quantum physics, which suggests that the act of observation affects the observed reality, has important implications when viewed through a spiritual lens. It hints at the power of consciousness – both in our humanity and primordial state – to influence the fabric of reality.

From this perspective, we can understand Yahweh as the ultimate Observer, whose divine consciousness and intention continually brings the universe into being. Our own consciousness, made in the image of Yahweh, participates in this ongoing act of creation through our thoughts, intentions and observations.

GEMSTONES AS CONDUITS OF DIVINE FREQUENCY

From a son of God's perspective, gemstones can be understood as crystallised forms of divine frequency. With this statement, I want to suggest that gemstones hold a unique place in God's creation serving as physical manifestations of spiritual realities. Each stone, with its unique molecular structure and elemental composition, resonates with specific celestial frequencies making it a conduit for particular aspects of glorious energy.

The concept of gemstones carrying specific frequencies is rooted in the understanding that all matter is, at its core, vibrating energy. The unique atomic structure of each gemstone creates a specific vibrational signature which interacts with the human energy field and the surrounding environment. Just as Elijah perceived the presence of God in a gentle whisper, while being in the cleft of the rock, those attuned to the subtle energies of gemstones may perceive their unique vibrational qualities.

GEMSTONES AND THE HUMAN ENERGY FIELD

The human body, created in the image of God, is not just a physical entity but also an energetic one for we are as God is and God is Spirit.

> "For God is a Spirit, and He longs to have sincere worshipers who adore Him in the realm of the Spirit and in truth." John 4:24 TPT

In the spiritual as well as the scientific field, there is a clear recognition of the existence of a subtle energy field surrounding the physical body. This energy field, also called the biometric field or, according to what I understand, the 'arche', (the spiritual estate or realm that you have stewardship over) is influenced by and responsive to different frequencies.

Gemstones, with their stable crystalline structures, emit consistent, coherent vibrational frequencies that can interact with the human energy field. This interaction affects your energetic balance and, if utilised correctly, can facilitate physical and emotional healing. Even deeper than that, it can facilitate breakthrough and you receiving your spiritual inheritance as with the tribes of Israel - the main purpose for me writing this book. As living stones we have been blessed and equipped with amazing technology to have these concepts actualised in our spirit as well as the realms we steward and to call forth the manifestation of God's promises. We have been called as a company of sons to manifest His victory and establish the new Jerusalem in the earth realm just as it is established in us through the cross.

Beyond their effects on individual human energy fields, gemstones are thought to influence the broader environment. This is the proof of our pre-destined call to stewardship where the sons of Yahweh are called to care for, harmonise and redeem creation.

> "The entire universe is standing on tiptoe, yearning to see the unveiling of God's glorious sons and daughters! For against its will the universe itself has had to endure the empty futility resulting from the consequences of human sin. But now, with eager expectation, all creation longs for freedom from its slavery to decay and to experience with us the wonderful freedom coming to God's children. To this day we are aware of the universal agony and groaning of creation, as if it were in the contractions of labor for childbirth."
> Romans 8:19-22 TPT

Large crystals or geodes placed in a space are believed to help cleanse and balance the energy of that environment. This practice is based on the idea that the consistent frequency emitted by the gemstone can help to neutralise discordant energies and create a more harmonious atmosphere.

THE SCIENCE AND SPIRITUALITY OF GEMSTONE FREQUENCIES - BRIDGING SCIENTIFIC UNDERSTANDING AND SPIRITUAL INSIGHT

Whilst the celestial properties of gemstones are not widely recognised by mainstream science, there are some interesting areas where scientific understanding and spiritual beliefs intersect.

Piezoelectricity, a property exhibited by some stones where they generate an electric charge in response to mechanical stress (same energetic response in the human body), demonstrates a tangible link between physical structure and energy. This phenomenon, discovered by science, seems to echo the spiritual belief in stones as energy transformers. Similarly, the ability of stones to oscillate at very precise frequencies (as utilised in quartz watches) hints at their capacity to maintain stable vibrational states - a quality central to their purported celestial properties.

QUANTUM ENTANGLEMENT AND NON-LOCAL EFFECTS

The concept of quantum entanglement, where particles remain connected so that actions performed on one affect the other, even at great distances, provides a scientific framework for understanding how gemstones might have non-local effects.

From a spiritual perspective this phenomenon can be seen as a reflection of the omnipresence of divine consciousness. Just as entangled particles remain connected across space, gemstones might be understood as maintaining a connection to their pre-coded heavenly information, channeling specific aspects of God's frequency regardless of their location - hence the ability for the precious stones' in the high priest's ephod to translate information from the spiritual realms into the earth system and into the tribes. Science can now prove gemstone's unique capacity to retain information for millions of years.

SACRED GEOMETRY AND TECHNOLOGICAL ROTATION DEVICES

Sacred geometry is a concept that has fascinated mystics, philosophers and even physics for millennia. At its core, sacred geometry posits that certain geometric patterns and proportions are imbued with spiritual significance and reflect fundamental principles of the cosmos. Mystic sages throughout history have revered these forms as keys to understanding the nature of reality and our place within it.

From my understanding, sacred geometric patterns act as a spiritual map or matrix with nodule points that intersect. In my personal exploration of these patterns, I have come to the conclusion that these patterns form a grid and the lines that run across are energy or ley lines or, more accurately, information lines.

Interestingly, the definition of a ley line is: *'a supposed straight line connecting three or more prehistoric or ancient sites, sometimes regarded as the line of a former track and associated by some with lines of energy or spiritual essence.'*

"Regarded as a line of a former track" speaks of a record of information coded or programmed into the line.

Where two of the information lines meet and overlap a nodule point is formed and acts as an energy generator. In other words, if every line is charged or coded with a specific energy (this includes information), and two energies meet, the frequency will be amplified. If the frequency wave is strong enough it collapses and this forms substance in the earth.

Many are sceptical of sacred geometry due to the connection with witchcraft and occult practices. I want to clearly state that land, stones and technologies can be usurped and defiled, but there are many treasures and unclaimed inheritances belonging to the sons of God that have been hi-jacked by the ungodly and I firmly believe we are called to claim the spoils of war back for the Kingdom of Light and restore the desolations of generations. You might feel sceptical in engaging geometry but I encourage you to lean into the revelation that the original architecture thereof came from heaven.

Sacred geometry was incorporated into the design of temples, cathedrals and other holy sites to create spaces that resonated with divine energy. Geometry reflects mathematical principles. While this metaphysical view may seem at odds with modern scientific understanding, there are some intriguing areas of overlap and support from scientific fields:

1. Mathematics and physics: The golden ratio and Fibonacci sequence appear with surprising frequency in nature, from the spiral of galaxies to the arrangement of leaves on plants. While their perceived aesthetic appeal may be subjective, their recurrence points to underlying mathematical principles at work in the physical world.

2. Cymatics: The study of visible sound and vibration has shown that certain frequencies produce geometric patterns in water or sand that resemble some sacred geometry forms. This demonstrates a connection between vibration, form and mathematical ratios.

3. Quantum physics: Some interpretations of quantum mechanics propose that geometric forms represent fundamental patterns in the quantum foam of spacetime. While highly speculative, this shows how cutting-edge physics can sometimes align with ancient mystical concepts.

4. Neuroscience: Studies have shown that the human brain responds positively to certain proportions and patterns, including the golden ratio. This may help explain the purported meditative effects of sacred geometry.

5. Crystallography: The study of crystal structures reveals naturally occurring geometric forms, including the Platonic solids, lending credence to the idea that these shapes are fundamental to nature.

6. Fractal geometry: The self-similar patterns found in fractals echo the nested, repeating forms of sacred geometry. Fractals are now recognised as a key principle in understanding natural forms and complex systems.

The persistence of sacred geometry across cultures and religious fields and its echoes in scientific discoveries suggest that these patterns may indeed reflect something fundamental about the structure of our physical and metaphysical universe.

As I mined this concept for better understanding, I perceived an image of a spirit body with a rotation device built into the centre of the chest area. I saw the 12 precious stones placed in the device and mechanisms that shifted the stones into different geometric patterns. It was clear to me this technology enables us to use the stones with different algorithms - each sequence delivering a specific result.

As we conclude our exploration of frequency, quantum fields and the spiritual properties of gemstones, we are left with a sense of the intricate and beautiful design of creation. From the subatomic realm to the cosmic scale we see evidence of Yahweh's divine symphony - a grand composition of frequencies orchestrated by the Creator.

Frequency, as we have discovered, is far more than a physical phenomenon. It is a fundamental aspect of existence - a means by which God communicates with us and creation. Gemstones, in this context, can be understood as unique expressions of supernatural frequency and crystallised forms of specific celestial energies.

Even greater than understanding physical attributes of certain precious stones is the revelation that we possess these treasures as part of our primordial make-up and design. Yeshua has grafted us into Himself and has merged Himself as the ultimate cornerstone with us. When we connect frequency and algorithms with each other, we will see certain results and these results can alter our lives as well as our governance.

CHAPTER 4

Heavenly blueprints, formulas and angelic assistance

Now that we have laid a firm foundation in understanding algorithms, frequency and some other technological concepts, let's weave it all together with the aim of understanding how the precious stones mentioned in the Word of Yahweh form part of our Kainos make-up and design.

There are four precious stone patterns or blueprints, if you will, in the Word that caught my attention and sparked the curiosity that led to writing this book. The first is the most common scripture referencing the stones, which is the high priest's ephod and the inlaying of the stones in a specific order, representing the tribes also in this particular order. The next connecting pattern was the instructions regarding the layout of the tribes around the tabernacle, described in Numbers 2:3. Then the Word explains the order in which the tribes had to move when they possessed the promised land, Canaan. Lastly, there is John's vivid depiction of the foundations of the New Jerusalem, made up of precious stones in a specific sequence. When you study each of these references you will find that the pattern or order of the stones and tribes were not static, but interchanged. This led me to seek understanding regarding Yahweh's methodology, since He is not a God who does things without purpose. So why change the order?

I experienced Holy Spirit instructing me in the intricacies of divine algorithms, explaining how each pattern corresponded to a specific heavenly mathematical equation. These formulas, I learned, were designed to yield particular outcomes or results not only in the spiritual realms but also in the physical.

In this orchestration, God has appointed facilitators - angelic beings and the 22 living letters (the tangible manifestation of God's word) to oversee these formulas, ensuring their fruition. Angelic intervention serves as a ministry to us.

> *"Are not all the angels ministering spirits sent out by God to serve those who will inherit salvation?"* Hebrews 1:14 AMP

Angels are mandated to be our helpers, executing assignments on our behalf and partnering with us to actualise the Word of God.

Among these divine facilitators is Pulmona, the angel of algorithms and mathematics. This being possesses the extraordinary ability to recalibrate and facilitate the coding within our spirit and primordial body's intricate technology, of which the stones form part of. The heavenly information or coding can then cascade through our soul and ultimately manifest in our physical body, enabling us to see the fruits of our spiritual inclinations.

We can also interface with the living letters—vibrational entities that resonate at specific frequencies, collapsing and manifesting the words released by Yahweh into our material world. These letters, being the Word in action, and the angels, in constant communion with Yeshua, are imbued with His divine light and assist us in activating divine technologies.

The 22 letters of the AlephBet were not mere linguistic symbols, but were imbued with profound spiritual significance. As mentioned in the previous chapter, the living letters are understood to be the very building blocks of creation, the primal building blocks through which the Almighty brought the universe into being. The letters emerged from Yahweh's essence as living, conscious entities - each possessing its own unique energetic quality, symbolic meaning and mystical power. They are not simply an abstract language but are seen as living, dynamic expressions of the divine creative force.

The living letters are believed to be the medium through which God spoke the world into existence:

> *"And then God announced, "Let there be light," and light burst forth!" Genesis 1:3 TPT*

This divine utterance is understood to have manifested through the strategic combination and permutation of the 22 sacred letters. Each letter was associated with a particular numerical value, astrological correspondence and divine attribute.

In the ancient Hebrew worldview, the 22 letters are not merely linguistic tools, but are living, sentient expressions of the divine creative intelligence - the building blocks through which Yahweh spoke the cosmos into being.

When we engage with our heavenly partners, they release the sound and light frequencies of Yeshua with which they are charged,

> Among these divine facilitators is Pulmona, the angel of algorithms. This being possesses the extraordinary ability to reorganise and facilitate the coding within our spirit's intricate technology.

energising our very being. These entities possess the ability to charge and energise the precious stones embedded in our spiritual temple. The stones, acting as spiritual conduits, absorb the light and sound frequencies, thereby altering their intrinsic coding and receiving the divine record. This process activates the formula within us causing light to radiate from our innermost being, transforming us into beacons of divine energy and affecting all that we steward and govern over.

Chrysolite

Emerald Sardius

Onyx Garnet

Lapis Lazuli

Agate

Amethyst Amber

Jasper Beryl

Sardonyx

Algorithm for Worship & Intercession

Images of stones used in this diagram are for illustrative purposes and creatively represents the actual stones.

Chapter 4 - Heavenly blueprints, formulas and angelic assistance | 47

CHAPTER 5
Algorithm of Worship and Intercession

Let's start with the first algorithm - one I understand as a formula for worship and intercession. The algorithm is the sequence of the stones placed in the breastplate of the high priest. We have been grafted into the order of Melchizedek of which Yeshua is the High Priest. This makes us priests and the garment which Yahweh instructed the Israelites to make and adorn the high priest with, has now been deposited into us.

(Disclaimer: there are numerous discrepancies as to which stones were actually used in the ephod. I have done as much research as I was able to, to try and present it as accurately as possible based on the locations, density, worth and translations of each of the precious stones mentioned. There will be other writings to likely differ from my findings and I might even gather new information to add to my current understanding, but as far as writing this piece, I feel confident in my interpretation.)

THE ARK OF THE COVENANT - AN ENERGY GENERATOR

The Ark of the Covenant, the most revered of Biblical relics, seems to have been far more complex than we have understood until now. It was a pivotal artefact in the tabernacle for the high priest to enter past the veil into the Holy of Holies and receive God's forgiveness, released from the mercy seat, for the tribes. There is a theory that the Ark may have served as a sophisticated frequency generator, maintaining a constant spiritual resonance within the tabernacle and, later, the temple.

This theory suggests that the Ark's unique construction - acacia wood overlaid with pure gold, crafted to precise specifications - was crucial to its function as an energy or frequency generator. The gold, being an excellent conductor, could have amplified and projected this energy. Even more intriguing is one of the contents of the Ark: the tablets of the Ten Commandments. These stone tablets, most likely to have been crystalline in nature, might have acted as natural oscillators.

The precious stones in the high priest's ephod each carried their unique vibrational properties. The specific arrangement of these stones on the breastplate was not arbitrary, but crucial for their collective resonance. Each stone was positioned to interact specifically with the Ark's frequency. When the high priest entered the Holy of Holies wearing this breastplate, an energetic event occurred. The Ark's continuous frequency, generated throughout the year, would interact with the resonant frequencies of the breastplate stones. This interaction caused an "arcing" effect - a visible or energetic connection between the Ark and the breastplate. The combined frequencies of the Ark and the precisely tuned stones created a harmonic resonance, dramatically amplifying the overall energy in the sacred space.

This amplified frequency, born from the marriage of the Ark's energy and the vibrations of the precious stones, is believed to have been capable of opening a direct portal or gateway to the heavenly realm. Specifically, it might have altered the priest's physical body to such an extent that he could trans-relocate through the veil - which could not be torn or separated, hence the awe when it happened at Yeshua's crucifixion - and granted him access into the true, celestial Holy of Holies.

This perspective presents the Ark and the high priest's regalia not just as symbolic items but as sophisticated spiritual technologies. It suggests an ancient understanding of frequency, energy and inter-dimensional communication that was encoded in temple practices and the precious stones.

WORSHIP AND INTERCESSION

The primary role of the high priest was to offer Yahweh pure worship and to intercede for the nations for justice and mercy. This too is our role as sons of God and co-heirs with Christ. We are to offer God our purest and most authentic worship because He is worthy of our adoration and wonder. Through Yeshua, we have become the precious stones and we now have the breastplate inside of us. As mentioned before, we have been equipped with rotation devices that can shift the stones into place in our spirit so we too can live in the Holy of Holies - not enter once a year as the priests did - but remain in that space of ecstatic union and worship.

Precious stones serve as powerful conduits in elevating worship, acting as sacred bridges between the earthly and divine realms. Just as the high priest's breastplate was adorned with specific stones ordained by God, each carrying unique spiritual frequencies, the stones we carry can amplify our worship in profound ways.

The living stones resonate with heaven's frequencies, much like crystal resonates with sound. When we incorporate them into our worship, they can help attune our spirit to higher spiritual vibrations. Think of them as sacred tuning forks, helping us align more precisely with heaven's wavelengths. Each stone carries its own divine signature. Some might amplify peace during contemplative worship, while others might strengthen our prophetic perception as we minister before the Lord. Like the stones in Solomon's temple, they can create an atmosphere that enhances our awareness of God's presence.

These stones don't generate power themselves - rather, they act as amplifiers of the Holy Spirit's movement, much like a prism breaks white light into its component colours. They help us perceive and interact with different aspects of God's nature more clearly during worship.

When we worship with understanding of these principles, precious stones can help create sacred space, amplify our spiritual sensitivity, and deepen our connection with the divine presence. They become tools that help us enter more fully into the courts of heaven, enhancing our ability to perceive and respond to God's presence. This algorithm, when activated, also enables for intercession. It vibrates at a level of intercession and mercy that Yeshua Himself established on the cross. Yeshua's contention for forgiveness and reconciliation altered the natural elements to such an extent that the weather conditions changed and the clouds were charged with thunder. The earth responded and the veil tore due to the frequency in His voice when He declared, "It is DONE!"

> "Jesus passionately cried out, took His last breath, and gave up His spirit. At that moment the veil in the Holy of Holies was torn in two from the top to the bottom. The earth shook violently, rocks were violently split apart," Matthew 27:50-51 TPT

If we want our prayers and worship to impact the earth and all we steward, then heavenly intervention is welcomed and crucial. We need to grasp our spiritual reality of being seated in heavenly places and being ambassadors and governors of the Kingdom of heaven. Our intercession has to be effective to shift chaos into order. Yeshua established the Kingdom INSIDE of us and commissioned us to establish and expand it on earth and make every other kingdom inoperative. Our prayers need to affect nations. It has to shift our consciousness into the heavenly realities and as we behold the functioning of God's realm, we are assigned to feed that into the earth and connect the realms - so what is below will mirror what is above. Enabling the living stones inside our spirit body to resonate with the original coding of the breastplate offers us abilities to successfully mandate this vision and actualise it in our earthly realities.

Application of this Algorithm

- Intercession and Worship
- Contending for breakthrough for others
- Activating joy
- Ascending into the Holy of Holies

Meditation Guideline to Activate the Algorithm of Worship and Intercession

Close your eyes and enter into the presence of Yeshua, our eternal High Priest. Take three deep breaths, each breath drawing you closed to His holy presence. Feel His Spirit of intercession beginning to move within you.

Become aware of the sacred stones within you, precious jewels that Yeshua Himself has placed in your being. Like the breastplate Aaron wore as he interceded for Israel, these stones hold divine purpose. See Yeshua's hands gently shifting them, realigning each one according to heaven's perfect pattern within you.

Listen now for His voice-that eternal song of intercession before the Father. Let His worship wash over your living stones like waves of glory. His pure light and heavenly harmonies flow through you, awakening each stone to its holy purpose. Watch as they begin to illuminate with His light, charging the same divine energy that files the throne room of heaven.

These are the very frequencies of His perpetual intercession. Feel Yeshua's own prayer life merging with yours. As your inner stones activate, they attune to His perfect worship. Divine capabilities transfer from His heart to yours - the very essence of how He communes with the Father now flowing through your earthly vessel and consciousness.

See the living letters appearing, arcing between the stones like bridges of living light. These are the eternal characters of heaven's language, moving in perfect harmony with Yeshua's intercession. Together they form sacred geometries of worship, as He draws you deeper into the Holy of holies where he ever lives to make intercession.

Join now with Yeshua's eternal ministry of worship. Let your praise rise pure and true to Yahweh, carried on the wings of His perfect intercession. Feel your entire being-stones, letters, body, and spirit-unified with Christ's own offering before the Father.

Your worship merges with his, becoming one pure symphony of adoration. Rest here in this divine alignment, knowing you are established in His presence. Let His high priestly ministry continue to work within you, purifying and elevating your worship through His perfect meditation. You stand now where He stands, in the very holy of holies, your prayers unified with His eternal intercession.

Take three more deep breaths, allowing this sacred union with Christ's intercession to settle deeply within you. When you are ready, slowly return to your awareness to your surroundings, carrying this divine alignment and the reality of your union with Yeshua's ministry before the Father.

Algorithm for the Trading Floor

Images of stones used in this diagram are for illustrative purposes and creatively represents the actual stones.

CHAPTER 6
Algorithm of the Trading Floor

The next algorithm we'll examine is based on the arrangement around the tabernacle during the Israelites' time in the desert. This specific configuration placed the tribe of Levi at the centre, encircled by the other 12 tribes. Interestingly, at this point, the 12 tribes actually comprised 13 houses due to the division of Joseph's house into Ephraim and Manasseh. Both of these new tribes maintained their connection to their father's house stone - the sardonyx.

It's important to note that while the high priest's breastplate contained only 12 stones, every subsequent algorithm includes 13 stones, accounting for the double sardonyx stones. This detail is particularly relevant to us, as we are referred to as the 13th tribe.

The original 12 tribes of the first covenant represented Yahweh's governmental blueprint for humanity and the earth under Adam's lineage. But the new covenant established a new order, transferring the government of the Kingdom to Yeshua's shoulders. Through this transition, Yeshua united all 12 tribes and 13 houses within Himself. As Kainos beings (new creations) and the first fruits of the second Adam (Yeshua), we have claimed possession of all 12 tribes. This makes us the 13th and final tribe, granting us access to the inheritance and blessings of all the tribes.

Understanding the gematria (numerical values) of Hebrew letters reveals additional significance: The sardonyx stone has a numerical value of 3 according the Hebraic gematria. The number 3 is associated with the Hebrew letter Gimmel (ג) symbolising the facilitation and distribution of resources from heavenly storehouses into our sphere of governance.

Therefore:

Double sardonyx = Double Gimmel (ג) = Double portion and provision. This symbolic equation suggests that our identity as the 13th tribe, represented by the double sardonyx, implies a divine promise of amplified blessings and heavenly resources.

Trading stands as a fundamental principle in the Kingdom of God. It's crucial to acknowledge that trading is a legitimate concept according to the Bible and has to be understood that we are not buying from God; rather, we are partnering with Him and stewarding assets. This perspective shifts our understanding from a transactional relationship with Yahweh to one of collaboration and responsible governing and stewardship; since we are already part of His household and there is no need for us to trade our way into the Kingdom. Yeshua accomplished the ultimate trade and He walked away the highest bidder - claiming all of humanity as His rightful possession.

Trading is a complex and multifaceted concept. It involves various commodities, including money, time, knowledge and seed and certainly does not limit commodities such as life essence, prayers and covenantal agreements - each of these holding high value. Moreover, there are several spiritual trading floors accessible to those who understand these principles.

Given this complexity, the importance of understanding what you are trading for cannot be overstated. In the spiritual realm, the heavens belong to the highest bidder, emphasising the need for discernment and wisdom in our spiritual transactions. This principle underscores the weight of our choices and the potential impact of our spiritual investments. Trading in the spiritual realm correlates closely with the Kingdom principles of sowing and reaping. Just as sowing into defiled or ungodly soil results in a compromised harvest, trading on ungodly floors leads to corrupted outcomes. This parallel highlights the importance of the spiritual environment in which we conduct our transactions. The stakes are high in this realm of trading, as generational blessings can either be claimed for a thousand generations or be inadvertently traded away through unwise trading and ungodly agreements.

THE TRIBAL LAYOUT: A BLUEPRINT FOR HEAVENLY TRADING

The arrangement of tribes around the tabernacle in ancient Israel provides a glorious picture of the nature of heavenly trading floors. At the centre of this layout was the tribe of Levi, symbolising active intercession and mercy at the core of all energetic transactions. Within this central space, the sacrificial altar was placed, representing Yeshua as the ultimate offering. In the spiritual economy, Yeshua's blood is the most valuable commodity across all realms. Its significance transcends mere symbolism; it actively speaks on behalf of the sons of God. The power of this sacrifice resonates from the altar at the centre of the trading floor, influencing every transaction and negotiation that takes place. This elevates our participation on the trading floors, grounding it in the supreme act of divine love and sacrifice. This central sacrifice grants us access to enter His courts, undefiled and righteous, approaching God's trading floors with purity and divine approval, for Yahweh is fully satisfies because of Chris's sacrifice.

Understanding these principles of Kingdom trading enables us to engage more effectively and responsibly in trading transactions. By recognising the value of Yeshua's sacrifice and the importance of trading on Godly floors, sons of God can ensure that our spiritual investments yield righteous and blessed returns. This approach to spiritual trading not only aligns with Biblical principle but also opens up avenues for profound growth and influence in both the seen and unseen realms.

When we engage our living stone technology to shift the stones into order according to the divine blueprint for trading, heavenly trading routes get activated. These trading routes open up to the infinite possibility for spiritual essence to transform into physical substance. Precious stones play a vital role in spiritual trading, acting as divine conductors of heaven's abundance and favour. Like sacred antennas tuned to heaven's frequencies, the living stones can be charged and activated to attract and channel spiritual commodities from the trading floors of heaven. When properly aligned, they function as magnetic centres that draw down divine provision, much like the Urim and Thummim were used to receive divine guidance and blessing. The stones can be programmed with specific biblical promises and declarations, creating a resonant field that interfaces with heaven's economy. Just as a crystal can conduct and amplify energy, the precious stones conduct and amplify the flow of spiritual blessings, creating bridges between heavenly storehouses and earthly manifestation. When activated during times of spiritual trading, they help establish stronger connections with heaven's trading floors, enabling clearer transactions and more efficient transfers of spiritual commodities into the natural realm. Like the precious stones in the foundations of the New Jerusalem, each one carries specific frequencies that can be aligned with different aspects of God's abundance, making them powerful tools for those who understand how to engage with heaven's economic systems.

Application of this Algorithm

- Business transactions and promotion
- Gifting and anointing
- Imparting blessings
- Financial trading and sowing
- Intercession and Fasting

Meditation Guideline to Activate the Algorithm of Heavenly Trading Floors

Center yourself in shalom and still any noise in your mind and heart by drawing your focus to Yeshua's beauty. Take three deep breaths, each one drawing you closer to divine awareness.

Feel and see the living stones within your being. These sacred jewels begin to vibrate and glow, awakening to their divine purpose. Sense them as they slowly rotate, each turning according to heaven's perfect design. Like stars aligning in their celestial dance, these stones move in harmony with the trading floors of heaven.

Now, envision these stones transforming into divine magnets. Feel their powerful attractive force activating within you. See streams of heavenly abundance and divine favour being drawn to you, flowing towards you like rivers of golden light. Each stone pulses with magnetic resonance, calling forth the blessings of the Lord.

Declare with confidence: "I am blessed and highly favoured by Yahweh."

Let these words resonate through every fibre of your being.

See yourself standing on the trading floors of the spirit. Above you unfurls a banner bearing the ancient promise: "The Lord will command the blessing on you in your storehouses and in all to which you set your hand" (Deuteronomy 28:8).

Feel this truth settling deep within you. Everything you touch is blessed with prosperity. Your hands carry divine potential. Your steps align with heaven's abundance.

Envision yourself positioned in the very centre of God's abundance. Like a tree planted by rivers of living water, your roots go deep into divine provision. Feel the flow of blessing moving through you, around you, emanating from you.

Declaration: "I am positioned in the abundance of God. Everything I touch prospers according to His divine plan."

Let the living stones continue their sacred rotation, each turn amplifying these truths within you. Feel yourself becoming a conductor of heaven's prosperity, a channel of divine favour.

Take three deep breaths to seal these alignments. Each breath anchors you more firmly in this place of commanded blessing.

When you are ready, slowly return to normal awareness, carrying within you these activated stones, these magnetic centres of divine abundance.

Garnet
Beryl
Amethyst
Amber
Sardius
Chrysolite
Jasper
Onyx
Lapis Lazuli
Agate
Sardonyx
Sardonyx
Emerald

Algorithm for Inheritance

Images of stones used in this diagram are for illustrative purposes and creatively represents the actual stones.

Chapter 6 - Algorithm of the Trading Floor | 63

CHAPTER 7
Algorithm of Inheritance

> *"Those who love Me gain great wealth and a glorious inheritance, and I will fill their lives with treasures."*
> Proverbs 8:21 TPT

I firmly believe that we, as followers of Christ, have access to a magnificent inheritance that is already within our reach. This inheritance, far from being a distant promise, is a present reality that we can claim and experience daily and inter-dimensionally.

In the realm of inheritance, as in the natural world, a death is necessary for an inheritance to be released. In our case, this death has already occurred. Yeshua willingly offered His life, fully embracing death before triumphantly overcoming it through His resurrection. This profound act serves as the cornerstone of our inheritance, not only in the spirit but also in what we are called to govern and steward on earth.

Yeshua's death was certified in both the earthly and spiritual realms and provides us with irrefutable evidence to support our claim on our inheritance. His death wasn't merely an earthly event; it was a concrete reality acknowledged across dimensions. This certification solidifies our right to the full spectrum of blessings and promises that comprise our spiritual legacy.

Yeshua's death serves a dual purpose. It enables us to receive the fullness of our inheritance and union in Him. Through His sacrifice, we gain access to a complete and unrestricted spiritual legacy. Also, it completely did away with the first created man, Adam's, fallen nature. As a result, we now live as Kainos beings, new creations fundamentally transformed at the core of our being.

Ultimately, all of this – Christ's death, our inheritance and our transformation – was orchestrated for Yeshua to receive His own full reward. This reward is the reconciliation of His image back to Himself, fully unified with His creation. In our transformation and reception of our inheritance, Christ sees the fulfilment of His sacrifice and the completion of His divine plan.

Our inheritance in Christ is not a distant hope by which death is our gateway into receiving the glory; but rather a present reality, made possible through His death and resurrection. Yeshua annihilated death and the sting thereof. For us, this means we should experience no form of lack or death in our earthly existence. Our soul, body, emotions, relationships, businesses, ministries and even finances should flourish as death and decay are removed from what we steward. Governing our realms of influence should code our environment with the glory of resurrection! As we grasp the magnitude of this truth, we

> Yeshua's death wasn't merely an earthly event; it was a concrete reality acknowledged across dimensions. This certification solidifies our right to the full spectrum of blessings and promises that comprise our spiritual legacy.

can live in the fullness of what Christ has secured for us, embracing our identity as new creations and participating in the divine unity that was Christ's ultimate goal.

Precious stones serve as living conductors of both heavenly frequencies and ancient inheritance, particularly connecting us to the divine legacies of the 12 tribes. The living stones attune us to the spiritual inheritance encoded within each tribal lineage. Each stone resonates with unique aspects of tribal blessing. When these stones are properly activated, they function as bridges not only between heaven and earth but also between present and past, allowing us to access the accumulated spiritual wealth of our forefathers in faith. Like sacred keys unlocking ancient storehouses, they help us interface with the specific blessings and divine mandates carried within each tribal lineage.

These living stones are programmed to resonate with specific tribal frequencies, creating channels through which ancient covenantal blessings can flow into our present reality. The stones serve as conductors of tribal wisdom and authority. When activated during ascension they help establish stronger connections with the generational blessings stored in heaven's vaults, enabling clearer transmission of spiritual inheritance into our spheres of influence.

Each stone carries unique vibrational patterns that correspond to different aspects of spiritual blessing. By understanding and engaging with the stones' specific frequencies, we can more fully step into our portion of inheritance, accessing not just general blessing but the particular grace and authority to govern it.

The stones act as crystalline matrices that can store and transmit information and frequencies, much like ancient memory banks holding the spiritual DNA of our forebears in faith. When properly aligned and activated, they create a resonant field that helps us interface with and manifest specific aspects of inheritance, transforming ancient promises into present-day reality.

INTERACTING WITH THE 12 TRIBES' BLESSINGS

Reuben: Embracing Stability and Integrity

> *"Reuben, my firstborn, you are my strength and the first fruits of my manhood. You are preeminent in pride and surpassing others in power. You are unstable—as turbulent as floodwaters; you will no longer excel, for you have slept with my concubine and defiled yourself in your father's bed!"*
> Genesis 49:3-4 TPT

Earthly Inheritance (Joshua 13:15-23): Territory east of the Jordan River, including parts of Gilead and the tableland from Aroer to Medeba.

Blessing Code: Potential for excellence; warring against instability.

Manifestation: Increased spiritual stability and moral integrity.

Simeon and Levi: Transforming Passion into Purpose

> *"Simeon and Levi, you are two of a kind and brothers in crime, for your swords have committed violent acts. O my soul, let me not join in their secret plans. O my heart, never let me be counted in their assembly, for they killed men in fits of rage, and for pleasure, they maimed an ox."* Genesis 49:5-6 TPT

Earthly Inheritance (Joshua 19:1-9): 48 Scattered cities within the territory of Judah.

Blessing Code: Transformation of scattered judgment into purposeful dispersion.

Manifestation: Redemption of personal weaknesses; broader spiritual influence.

Judah: Claiming Royal Priesthood

> *"O Judah, your brothers will praise you. You will conquer your foes in battle, And your father's sons will bow down before you. Judah, my son, you are like a young lion who has devoured its prey and departed. Like a lion, he crouches and lies down, and like a lioness—who dares to awaken him? The scepter of rulership will not be taken from Judah, nor the ruler's staff from his descendants, until the Shiloh comes and takes what is due him, for the obedience of nations belongs to him. He will tether his donkey to the vine and his purebred colt to the choicest branch. He will wash his garments in wine and his robe in the blood of grapes. His eyes are more exhilarating than wine and his teeth whiter than milk."*
> *Genesis 49:8-12 TPT*

Earthly Inheritance (Joshua 15:1-63): Large territory in the southern part of Canaan, including Jerusalem and Bethlehem.

Blessing Code: Royal authority and Messianic promise.

Manifestation: Advancing the government of God in the earth and claiming our position as kings, seated in heavenly realms. Increased sense of spiritual authority and purpose.

> *"But you are God's chosen treasure —priests who are kings, a spiritual "nation" set apart as God's devoted ones. He called you out of darkness to experience His marvellous light, and now He claims you as His very own. He did this so that you would broadcast His glorious wonders throughout the world."* 1 Peter 2:9 TPT

Zebulun: Bridging Worlds

Earthly Inheritance (Joshua 19:10-16): Territory in the north, between the Sea of Galilee and the Mediterranean Sea.

Blessing Code: Living at the crossroads, connecting different realms.

Manifestation: Enhanced ability to affect the atmosphere and transferring situations into Shalom. Being "in the world but not of it," and facilitating effective cultural engagement.

Issachar: Cultivating Spiritual Discernment

> "Issachar is a strong donkey lying down between its saddlebags. When he sees that his resting place is good, and his portion is so pleasant, then he will bend his shoulder to the burden and labor for his master." Genesis 49:14-15 TPT

Earthly Inheritance (Joshua 19:17-23): Fertile territory in the Jezreel Valley.

Blessing Code: Understanding times and seasons.

Manifestation: Greater authority to redeem time and re-align lifelines with timelines.

Dan: Contention

> "Dan will provide justice for his people as one of the tribes of Israel. Dan will be a snake waiting by the roadside, like a snake in the grass. He bites the horse's heels, making its rider fall backward." Genesis 49:16-17 TPT

Earthly Inheritance (Joshua 19:40-48): Initially in the south near the Philistines, later also in the far north of Israel.

Blessing Code: Executing judgment

Manifestation: Increased effectiveness in spiritual contentions and bringing order into chaos.

Gad: Developing Resilience

> "Gad will be raided by raiders, but he will raid at their heels and overcome them at last." Genesis 49:19 TPT

Earthly Inheritance (Joshua 13:24-28): Territory east of the Jordan

River, south of the half-tribe of Manasseh.

Blessing Code: Overcoming challenges, turning defense into offence.

Manifestation: Increased spiritual resilience, ability to thrive under pressure.

Asher: Cultivating Abundance and Generosity

> *"Asher's food will be rich, and he will provide delicacies fit for a king." Genesis 49:20 TPT*

Earthly Inheritance (Joshua 19:24-31): Coastal region in the northwest of Canaan.

Blessing Code: Richness of provision; ability to bless others.

Manifestation: Increased joy in giving an partnering with the Kingdom of Heaven

Naphtali: Embracing Freedom and Grace in Speech

> *"Asher's food will be rich, and he will provide delicacies fit for a king." Genesis 49:20 TPT*

Earthly Inheritance (Joshua 19:32-39): Mountainous region in the north, including the western shore of the Sea of Galilee.

Blessing Code: Freedom of spirit, beauty in expression.

Manifestation: Increased sense of freedom, grace-filled communication.

Joseph: Cultivating Fruitfulness Despite Adversity

> *"Joseph is a fruitful vine, a fruitful vine growing by a spring, whose branches run over a wall. Persecutors fiercely attacked him; they pursued him with their bow and arrows. But Joseph's bow remained steady, because the power of the Mighty One of Jacob strengthened him, by the name of the loving Shepherd, the Rock of Israel. The God of your father*

will help and protect you; the God who is more than enough will bless you. He will bless you with the blessings of heaven, blessings of the deep that lie beneath, and blessings of the breast and womb. The blessings of your father will be greater than the blessings of the eternal mountains, surpassing the blessings of my ancestors! May Joseph's blessings crown his head and rest on the brow of the one set apart, prince among his brothers." Genesis 49:22-26 TPT

EARTHLY INHERITANCE:

- Ephraim **(Joshua 16:5-10)**: Central hill country of Canaan.

- Manasseh **(Joshua 17:1-13)**: Territory both east and west of the Jordan River.

Blessing Code: Abundant fruitfulness, overcoming through divine help.

Manifestation: Resilience in trials, increased spiritual productivity.

Benjamin: Claiming Victory and Sharing Spoils

"Benjamin is a ferocious wolf. He devours his prey; in the evening, he divides the spoil."" Genesis 49:27 TPT

Earthly Inheritance (Joshua 18:11-28): Small but strategic area between Judah and Ephraim, including parts of Jerusalem.

Blessing Code: Taking the Kingdom by force, enjoying and sharing fruits of victory.

Manifestation: Boldness in faith.

The blessings and inheritances of the 12 tribes of Israel are not mere historical accounts but living spiritual legacies. As sons of God, we can interact with these blessings through the living stones and receive the predestined blessings coded into each of the tribes' records.

Application of this Algorithm

- Courts of Heaven
- Contending for land
- Transforming curse into blessing

Mediation Guideline to Activate the Algorithm of Inheritance

Settle into shalom, bringing your awareness to Yeshua's presence. Take three deep breaths, each one drawing you deeper into communion with Him.

Behold Yeshua, the source of every spiritual blessing, whose love flows boundlessly toward you. Feel His presence enveloping you like a mantle of light. In His radiance, become aware of the living stones within your spirit-these precious gifts He has placed within you.

Let your heart open to receive as you contemplate His words: "Every spiritual blessing..." Feel those living stones beginning to pulse with holy energy, each one awakening to its heavenly frequency. They are attenuating themselves to the very blessings of heaven, like instruments being perfectly tuned to a divine symphony.

Watch as light begins to emanate from your being. You are becoming a conduit of Christ's radiance.

From deep within, where the living stones reside, His light pours forth like a fountain of living water. This is not just light, but the vary Light of Christ flowing through you.

Now, bring to mind the situations you are contending for. See this holy light streaming from you toward these circumstances. The Light of Christ touches each situation, transforming the very atmosphere. Divine codes of blessing begin to rewrite earthly limitations.

Speak forth with confident authority: "I command the blessings of Yahweh to saturate these circumstances."

Feel the resonance of this declaration as it moves through the living stones within you. Watch as waves of blessing flow out, permeating every situation you've lifted up. Heaven's abundance merges with earth's reality where your faith stands guard.

Rest here in this place of divine interface-where your spirit, charged with heaven's blessings, becomes a gateway for Yahweh's abundance to flow. Let the Light of Christ continue to stream through you, transforming all it touches.

Take three deep breaths, sealing these holy alignments. Feel the living stones sustaining their heavenly resonance within you, maintaining this divine connection even as you return to normal awareness.

Carry this light with you, knowing that Yeshua's blessings continue to flow through the living stones of your spirit, saturating every circumstance you encounter and transforming you into a living stone itself.

Algorithm of Immortality

Images of stones used in this diagram are for illustrative purposes and creatively represents the actual stones.

Chapter 7 - Algorithm of Inheritance | 75

CHAPTER 8
Algorithm of Immortality

> *"We can all draw close to Him with the veil removed from our faces. And with no veil we all become like mirrors who brightly reflect the glory of the Lord Jesus. We are being transfigured into His very image as we move from one brighter level of glory to another. And this glorious transfiguration comes from the Lord, who is the Spirit."*
> 2 Corinthians 3:18 TPT

In redemption, Yeshua's sacrifice on the cross stands as a multifaceted masterpiece transcending far past forgiveness of sin and shame. Whilst this forgiveness is undoubtedly a priceless gift of grace - clothing us in His righteousness and granting us bold access to the heavenly realms - I believe the implications of His crucifixion and resurrection reach even further.

At its core, I am convinced that Christ's sacrifice not only pardoned our transgressions but fundamentally restored our spiritual image, eradicating the markers of the fall, death, and decay. This restoration was not an afterthought but a preordained plan with Yeshua as the Lamb slain before the world's foundation. Our redemption and salvation were recorded in the heavenly realms prior to earth's formation and Adam's creation.

Consider the profound implications of this timing. Whilst earthly events may be temporal and variable, what takes place in the eternal realms, i.e heaven, remains immutable. Sin acknowledged in eternity would persist eternally but so too would the forgiveness granted in these realms. Thus, Yeshua's pre-creation sacrifices released forgiveness and salvation throughout the heavens and across every dimension, stretching infinitely backward and forward in time, reconciling every spirit born of Yahweh back to Him through this eternal act of grace.

> Yeshua's pre-creation sacrifice released forgiveness and salvation throughout the heavens and across every dimension, stretching infinitely backward and forward in time, reconciling every spirit born of Yahweh back to Him.

Yet, for this reconciliation to have manifested in the earth and in our worlds - and by worlds I refer to our mind, soul, and emotions - the same record of forgiveness had to be established in the earth realm. This necessity explains Yeshua's humanity and His physical crucifixion. It was a cosmic alignment offering creation the same salvation already decreed in the heavenly records, bringing harmony between the upper and lower realms so that Yahweh's will might be done on earth as it is in heaven.

> "Manifest Your Kingdom realm, and cause Your every purpose to be fulfilled on earth, just as it is in Heaven."
> Matthew 6:10 TPT

In essence, Yeshua's work bridges the eternal and the temporal, the spiritual and the physical. It not only cleansed us from sin but proactively restores our nature, realigning us with Yahweh's original design. As we grasp the full scope of this redemption, we begin to understand the incredible glorification and transfiguration available to us—a transformation that touches every aspect of our being and extends to the very fabric of creation itself. We are called to embody this reconciliation, extending the eternal salvation we have gained into every corner of our terrestrial existence and partnering with heaven's agenda to remove death and all records thereof from the earth.

> "Then one of the seven angels who had the seven bowls full of the last seven plagues came to me and said, "Come. I will show you the beautiful bride, the wife of the Lamb." He carried me away in the realm of the Spirit to the top of a great, high mountain. There he showed me the holy city, Jerusalem, descending out of heaven from God. It was infused with the glory of God, and its radiance was like that of a very rare jewel, like a jasper, clear as crystal. It had a massive, high wall with twelve gates, and each gate had an angel. Each gate had written upon it a name of one of the twelve tribes of Israel— three gates on the east, three gates on the north, three gates on the south, and three gates on the west. The city wall had twelve foundations, and on them were the names of the twelve apostles of the Lamb."
> Revelation 21:9-14 TPT

> "The city was pure gold, clear as crystal, and its wall was made of jasper. The twelve foundations of the wall were adorned with every kind of precious stone—the first was jasper, the second sapphire, the third agate, the fourth emerald, the fifth onyx, the sixth carnelian, the seventh chrysolite, the eighth beryl, the ninth topaz, the tenth chrysoprase, the eleventh turquoise, and the twelfth amethyst. The twelve gates are twelve pearls—each gate made of one pearl. And the street of the city was pure gold, clear as crystal." Revelation 21:18-21 TPT

The Jasper stone represents the tribe of Benjamin, the youngest of all the brothers, and in all the previous algorithms or sequences he was either last or in the middle, yet in John's descriptive illustration, he vividly saw Benjamin's stone as the first layer of foundation in the wall of the glorified city, amplifying Yeshua's words that the last shall be first.

In the realm of the Kingdom we are one church, all unified, across generations and cultures. We are one in Christ and even us, as the sons at the closing of this age, will be considered to be first - on par with the saints that went before us.

I believe that every dispensation had its forerunners, pioneers and sons recoding the physical realm with heavenly information for the next to advance with. It is also my belief that we are not to wait for the destruction of earth in order for the remnant to go to her heavenly banquet with Yeshua. We are already seated at His banquet; already feasting on His faithfulness, for He has done all that He needed to do to redeem and He has bought back all that was traded away. We have been commissioned, from the very beginning of the ages, to restore the earth back to its original intent - Eden, partnering with Yeshua's pre-destined plan and agenda. Actualising all that He has placed within us to execute His Kingdom's laws and advance the government of the Kingdom of Light on earth. We are now at the culmination of the ages where all of creation turns to the **MANIFESTED** sons of Glory so that they - creation - can also receive the same salvation as the sons have - **FREEDOM!**

> *"The entire universe is standing on tiptoe, yearning to see the unveiling of God's glorious sons and daughters! For against its will the universe itself has had to endure the empty futility resulting from the consequences of human sin. But now, with eager expectation, all creation longs for freedom from its slavery to decay and to experience with us the wonderful freedom coming to God's children."* Romans 8:19-21 TPT

We are in an age where we are weaving together all the expressions of His goodness that were experienced throughout the dispensations and offer to Him the fullness of His reward... us! **Glorified, transformed, transfigured!**

The key to attaining immortality is to cultivate an unwavering conviction that death has no power over us. We must rise above the temporary trials and tribulations of this earthly existence and fix our gaze firmly on the eternal, deathless nature of our primordial selves.

Each trial we navigate, each system we redeem, is an opportunity to imprint the invincible energies of heaven and of Yeshua's victory onto the earth plane. As we do this, not only do we liberate ourselves from the grip of mortality, but we establish new paradigms where lack, destruction and death have no dominion.

The world and the generations that follow will then bear witness to this transformation, as we demonstrate through our very beings that true, lasting life is the rightful inheritance of the sons of God. This is the highest purpose we are called to - not just to survive, but to embody and radiate the immortal splendour that is our divine birthright in Christ.

DIVINE HEALTH

As sons of God our spirits are eternally seated in the heavenly realms, charged with the very light and energy of Yeshua. Yet in this dense, chaotic physical realm, our bodies can become tethered to the turbulence of stress, sorrow, and fear - draining our vital life force and leading to misalignment with the blueprint of perfect health.

But in beholding the finished work of our Yeshua we find the key to overcoming illness. By beholding the perfected, flawless nature of our spirit man, we interface with the divine algorithm of immortality - a framework for life that knows no end.

In this state of observation we subject our physical forms to the divine blueprint of the New Jerusalem, where we embody the fullness of what our Beloved traded His life to secure. For what we behold, we become - the quantum fibres of our being aligning with the incorruptible, primordial image we choose to fix our eyes upon.

As this immutable truth floods our souls, our very cells respond, reprogramming the body to the original design of wholeness and deathlessness. The living stones grafted into the fabric of our consciousness facilitate this information until our entire being exudes the immortal splendour that is our birthright.

TIME AND SPACE

To fully embody the immortal nature of our being, we must reclaim our rightful dominion over the flexible dimensions of space and time. These are not rigid constraints but malleable fabrics that can be stretched, compressed and reshaped according to the dictates of our consciousness. Though we may find imprints of traumatic experiences - painful events that have left indelible marks on the fabric of our reality - it is in recognising the fluid, non-linear nature of these dimensions that we find freedom. The recurring patterns of undesirable experiences, rooted in past traumas, does not need to confine us to endless loops of suffering. We are meant to be free from the limitations of time and space. The immortal essence of our primordial self transcends these parameters.

By aligning our vision with the eternal blueprint held in the mind of Christ, we are empowered to bridge the gap between our current position and our destined eternity. In this state of expanded awareness, we effectively pull the future into the present, transcending the conventional boundaries of linearity and manifesting the immortal splendour that is our rightful inheritance.

Through this shift in perspective our experiences become increasingly harmonised with the intentions of our Father for we have reclaimed our mastery over the very fabric of spacetime, weaving the tapestry of our lives with the unwavering threads of immortality and eternal life in Yeshua.

Application of this Algorithm

- Meditation and ascension
- Healing physical body
- Leaning in for divine downloads
- Healing and realigning timelines

Meditation Guideline to Activate the Algorithm of Immortality

Center yourself in the presence of the Resurrected One. Take three deep breaths, each breath drawing in the reality of eternal life-not a future promise, but a present inheritance flowing from Yeshua's victory.

Behold Him now, radiant in His glorified form. This is your Elder Brother, your forerunner into eternal life. Feel the profound truth settling into your spirit: your eternal life doesn't begin at death's threshold-it burst forth the moment He conquered death. It flows now, alive and active within you.

Become aware of your body as a living temple, every cell sanctified for God's dwelling. Feel divine light beginning to pulse through you, reaching into the deepest places of your being. The living stones within you respond to His life-light, each one shifting, realigning into heaven's sequence of eternal life. Watch as waves of resurrection power flow through your temple-body, soul, and spirit unified in His life.

From your innermost being, feel the streams of living water beginning to flow. Like a river of light, they surge outward, touching everything within your sphere of influence. See dead things reviving, dormant seeds sprouting, as His life extends through you into creation.

Let your eyes fix upon Yeshua's glorified face. As you behold Him, feel the stunning reality: death's sting dissolved, its power nullified. Death holds no claim over you. In Christ, you stand beyond its reach, already seated in heavenly places.

Feel the resonance of eternal life activating dormant abilities within your earthly frame. Your very cells begin to vibrate with resurrection frequencies. Like a tuning fork struck by heaven's hand, your being aligns with Christ's glorified image.

Declare with holy conviction: "As He is now, so am I."

Watch as your earthly existence begins to mirror His resurrected glory.

The same Spirit that raised Christ from the dead now dwells in you, transforming your mortal body with His eternal life. You are becoming a living expression of His victory over death and decay.

See the reality of salvation flowing from you into the creation around you. Every place your influence touches becomes infused with His life. Hope springs forth, renewal begins, restoration flows-all because the Eternal One lives within you.

Rest in this profound truth: you are not moving toward eternal life; you are moving from it. It flows from His victory, through your being, and into the world around you.

Take three deep breaths, sealing these revelations in your spirit. Your body is His temple, your being resonates with His life and death has lost its hold. Carry this eternal reality with you as you return to your surroundings,

High Priest's Ephod	Layout around Tabernacle	Possession of Canaan	Foundations of New Jerusalem
WORSHIP	TRADING FLOOR	INHERITANCE	IMMORTALITY
Ex. 28:15-21	Num. 2-3	Num. 10:29-36	Rev. 21:9-20
1st Row	NORTH (Camp of Dan)	Group 1	
Sardius (Reuben)	Lapis Lazuli (Dan)	Garnet (Judah)	Jasper (Benjamin)
Chrysolite (Simeon)	Agate (Asher)	Amethyst (Issachar)	Lapis Lazuli (Dan)
Emerald (Levi)	Onyx (Naphtali)	Beryl (Zebulun)	Agate (Asher)
2nd Row	EAST (Camp of Judah)	Group 2	
Garnet (Judah)	Garnet (Judah)	Sardius (Reuben)	Emerald (Levi)
Lapis Lazuli (Dan)	Amethyst (Issachar)	Chrysolite (Simeon)	Sardonyx (Joseph)
Onyx (Naphtali)	Beryl (Zebulun)	Amber (Gad)	Sardius (Reuben)
3rd Row	SOUTH (Camp of Reuben)	Group 3	
Amber (Gad)	Sardius (Reuben)	Sardonyx (Ephraim)	Garnet (Judah)
Agate (Asher)	Chrysolite (Simeon)	Sardonyx (Mannaseh)	Beryl (Zebulun)
Amethyst (Issachar)	Amber (Gad)	Jasper (Benjamin)	Chrysolite (Simeon)
4th Row	WEST (Camp of Ephraim)	Group 4	
Beryl (Zebulun)	Sardonyx (Ephraim)	Lapis Lazuli (Dan)	Onyx (Naphtali)
Sardonyx (Joseph)	Sardonyx (Mannaseh)	Agate (Asher)	Amber (Gad)
Jasper (Benjamin)	Jasper (Benjamin)	Onyx (Naphtali)	Amethyst (Issachar)
	CENTRE/ TEMPLE	Carrying the Ark	
	Emerald (Levi)	Emerald (Levi)	

CHAPTER 9

Properties of the 12 Precious Stones

Throughout this book, we've explored the divine beauty encoded within precious stones by Yahweh. The Bible provides a foundation for understanding these marvellous creations, from the breastplate of the high priest to the foundations of the New Jerusalem. Just as these gems adorn the earth, I propose that their original blueprint resides within us, waiting to be activated by the radiance of Christ's light. When interfaced with, these stones have the potential to transform key aspects of our lives and spheres of influence.

The stones in the earth were originally crafted to serve the sons of God, bridging the physical and spiritual realms. Building on this Biblical understanding, I've compiled an overview of these precious stones, integrating holistic references with emerging scientific research on their vibrational properties and interactions with the human body, mind and energy field. I also included their relationship with the living letters and how the letters interact with and release frequency through the stones.

LIVING LETTERS AND THEIR REPRESENTATION

Consonants

Letter	Name	Numerical Value	Represents
א	Aleph	1	Divine unity, primordial force, silent potential
ב	Bet	2	House, container, blessing, duality
ג	Gimmel	3	Movement, dynamic energy, giving/receiving
ד	Dalet	4	Door, pathway, humility
ה	Hey	5	Divine breath, revelation, presence
ו	Vav	6	Hook, connection, channel between heaven/earth
ז	Zayin	7	Sword, spiritual sustenance, time
ח	Chet	8	Life force, fence, protection
ט	Tet	9	Hidden good, womb, intrinsic wisdom
י	Yod	10	Divine point, spark of creation, wisdom
כ/ך	Kaf/Kaf Sofit	20	Palm, receiving vessel, potential
ל	Lamed	30	Teaching, direction, aspiration
מ/ם	Mem/Mem Sofit	40	Water, womb, wisdom
נ/ן	Nun/Nun Sofit	50	Fish, soul movement, faithfulness
ס	Samech	60	Support, circular motion, divine support
ע	Ayin	70	Eye, divine providence, insight
פ/ף	Peh/Peh Sofit	80	Mouth, expression, manifestation
צ/ץ	Tzade/Tzade Sofit	90	Righteous one, foundation, justice
ק	Qof	100	Holiness, back of head, transcendence
ר	Resh	200	Head, beginning, divine mind
ש	Shin	300	Divine fire, transformation, balance
ת	Tav	400	Truth, completion, seal

Vowel Points

Vowel	Name	Position	Represents
	Kamatz	Below	Fullness, completion
	Patach	Below	Opening, revelation
	Tzere	Below	Directed focus, intention
	Segol	Below	Three-fold harmony, balance
	Chirik	Below	Penetrating wisdom
	Cholam	Above	Elevation, spiritual ascent
	Kubutz	Below	Gathering, concentration
	Shva	Below	Rest, stability
	Chataf Patach	Below	Swift opening
	Chataf Segol	Below	Swift harmony
	Chataf Kamatz	Below	Swift fullness

Special Points

Point	Name	Usage	Represents
	Dagesh	Inside letter	Emphasis, intensification
	Shin dot	Above right	Right side activation
	Sin dot	Above left	Left side activation
	Rafe	Above	Softening

Note: Final forms (Sofit) of letters are used when the letter appears at the end of a word and often represent the completion or containment of that letter's energy.

STONE: EMERALD | BAREQET

Tribe: Levi

Frequency Range: 14,000 - 14,500 Hz

Hebrew writing: בָּרֶקֶת

בּ (Bet with dagesh) - The emphasised Bet represents a sacred container or house. In emerald, it creates a concentrated vessel for divine love and healing light. The dagesh (dot) intensifies its containing power, particularly for heart frequencies.

ר (Resh) - Represents divine mind/head but in emerald specifically channels creative love into heart wisdom. Works with the stone's ability to bridge the mind of Christ and heart consciousness.

ק (Qof) - Represents holiness and sanctification. In emerald, it specifically works with the stone's ability to sanctify and purify heart energy while reaching between higher and lower realms.

ת (Tav) - The final letter represents completion and truth. It seals and completes the heart healing circuit while grounding truth through love.

Together these letters create a sophisticated heart healing circuit: Bet contains the green ray, Resh channels divine love, Qof sanctifies heart energy and Tav completes healing pattern. The vowel points serve crucial functions: Kamatz fills with healing energy, double Segol creates perfect harmony and the combination maintains emerald's frequency.

This letter combination explains emerald's traditional properties:
- Healing trauma
- Divine love transmission
- Wisdom through heart
- Balance of higher/lower energies
- Truth through love

Together, these letters create a complete circuit: Bet contains the energy, Resh receives the divine frequency, Qof transforms it and Tav grounds it into manifestation. This explains why emerald has such powerful properties for heart healing, wisdom activation and spiritual growth - the very letters of its name create a cosmic technology for frequency modulation and healing transmission.

The letters don't just name the stone - they actively participate in its energetic properties. When you interact with an emerald, these Hebrew letters are constantly dancing in the quantum field around the stone, facilitating its healing properties and maintaining its unique frequency signature. This is why in ancient traditions, knowing the true name of something gave you access to its power - the letters themselves are living keys to the stone's spiritual technology.

PHYSICAL PROPERTIES

1. Physical healing:
- Supports the immune system
- Improves eyes and vision
- Aids in detoxification of the liver
- Associated with heart health and circulation

2. Emotional healing:
- Facilitates emotional balance
- Promotes harmony and unity
- Alleviates stress and anxiety
- Encourages compassion and empathy

3. Mental healing:
- Improves mental clarity
- Enhances memory and focus
- Promotes wisdom and patience
- Stimulates creativity and inspiration

4. Spiritual healing:
- Associated with God's love and connection
- Believed to promote truth and integrity

STONE: SARDIUS | ODEM

Tribe: Reuben

Frequency Range: *Not documented

Hebrew writing: אֹדֶם

א (Aleph) - The first letter of the Hebrew alphabet represents unity and divine creative force. As the first letter of the sardius name, it channels primordial energy and represents the stone's connection to the life force of Yeshua. Since sardius is known for its deep red colour, Aleph facilitates the stone's connection to vital energy and the Blood.

ד (Dalet) - Represents a door or portal, symbolising how the sardius stone opens pathways between different dimensions of consciousness. In the stone's matrix, Dalet helps facilitate transformation and movement of energy.

ם (Mem Sofit) - The final form of Mem represents water and the depths. As the closing letter it contains and circulates the stone's energy, much like blood in the body. It works with the stone's grounding and stabilising properties.

Together, these letters create a powerful frequency circuit: Aleph initiates the primal life force energy, the Cholam vowel above the Aleph represents the breath of life and elevation - elevating and refining this raw power, Dalet transforms and distributes the energy and final Mem contains and circulates it throughout the subtle bodies.

This letter combination explains why sardius has traditionally been associated with:

- Vitality and life force activation
- Blood purification and circulation
- Grounding and stabilising properties
- Transformation and renewal

The letters work together to maintain the stone's signature vibration with Aleph providing the initial spark, Dalet directing the energy flow and final Mem ensuring the energy remains contained and properly circulated. This creates a perfect balance of activation and stabilisation, making sardius particularly effective for working with physical vitality and spiritual transformation.

The red colour of the stone is directly connected to the name's lettering, as אדם also shares its root with "red" (אדום/adom) in Hebrew, showing how the living letters literally manifest the stone's physical appearance and energetic properties.

PHYSICAL PROPERTIES

1. Physical healing:
   - Improves blood circulation
   - Boosts energy and vitality
   - Aids in the absorption of vitamins and minerals
   - Associated with fertility and reproductive health

2. Emotional healing:
   - Considered a stone of courage and confidence
   - Promotes motivation and willpower
   - Alleviates feelings of anger or resentment
   - Encourages a positivity

3. Mental healing:
   - Enhances focus and concentration
   - Stimulates creativity and original thinking
   - Improves analytical abilities
   - Said to help in decision-making processes

4. Spiritual healing:
   - Considered a grounding and stabilising stone
   - Believed to enhance connection to the physical world

STONE: CHRYSOLITE | TARSHISH

Tribe: Simeon

Frequency Range: *Not documented

Hebrew writing: תַּרְשִׁישׁ

ת (Tav) - As the final letter of the Hebrew alphabet appearing at the beginning, represents perfect completion and truth. In chrysolite it initiates a complete circuit of manifestation helping the stone bridge celestial and earthly realms.

ר (Resh) - Symbolises head/beginning/cosmic consciousness. In chrysolite, it facilitates the stone's connection to the Spirit of Wisdom.

שׁ (Shin) - Appears twice in the name, representing divine fire and transformation. The first Shin processes spiritual light while the second grounds it. Together they create a purifying circuit within the stone.

י (Yod) - The divine spark or point of creation works with the stone's ability to manifest divine potential.

Together these letters create a sophisticated energy matrix: Tav initiates the complete circuit, Resh channels wisdom, the double Shin creates a transformative fire circuit and Yod activates divine potential. The vowel points play a crucial role in moderating and directing these powerful energies, ensuring the stone's frequency remains harmonious and accessible for human use.

This letter combination explains chrysolite's traditional properties:
- Transformation of higher wisdom into practical knowledge
- Balance between spiritual insight and earthly application

The double Shin is particularly significant, creating an internal purification circuit that helps chrysolite transmute negative energies and enhance strength. The placement of Tav at the beginning rather than end suggests this stone works backwards from completion to manifestation - helping you see the end result first, then bringing it into being.

PHYSICAL PROPERTIES

1. Physical healing:
- Aids in digestion and metabolism
- Supports liver function
- Detoxification of the body
- Alleviates physical exhaustion

2. Emotional healing:
- Considered a stone of compassion and harmony
- Reduces stress and irritability
- Helps overcome feelings of guilt or self-blame
- Promotes emotional balance

3. Mental healing:
- Facilitates mental clarity and focus
- Enhances learning and understanding
- Stimulates creativity and imagination
- Said to help in decision-making processes

4. Spiritual healing:
- Considered a stone of transformation and growth
- Associated with spiritual purification
- Thought to bridge the gap between the mind and the spirit

STONE: GARNET | NOPHECH

Tribe: Judah

Frequency Range: 1,050 - 1,200 Hz

Hebrew writing: נֹפֶךְ

נ (Nun) - Represents faith, seed and infusion of divine light into matter. As the first letter, it governs how the garnet draws down divine energy and facilitates spiritual transformation. Nun has a special connection to hidden light and potential, relating to the garnet's deep red glow.

פ (Peh) - Symbolises the mouth/speech and divine utterance. It works with the stone's expressive and manifestation properties, helping to articulate and direct its energies. It's also connected to breakthrough moments and revelation.

ך (Kaf Sofit) - The final form of Kaf represents the palm or container that holds blessing. As the closing letter, it cups and contains the garnet's powerful energies, allowing for proper distribution and grounding.

Together, these letters create a dynamic energy circuit: Nun initiates the descent of spiritual light, Peh transforms this light into manifesting power and final Kaf contains and distributes the energy. The vowel points play crucial roles: Cholam elevates the frequency and Segol balances the intense energies.

This letter combination explains garnet's traditional properties:
- Grounding spiritual energy into physical form
- Activation of life force and vitality
- Enhancement of creative expression
- Protection and containment of energy
- Manifestation of hidden potential

The letter structure explains garnet's reputation as a stone of manifestation and creative power - the letters literally create a circuit that draws down spiritual energy (Nun), articulates it into form (Peh) and contains it for practical use (Kaf Sofit).

PHYSICAL PROPERTIES

1. Physical healing:
- Boosts energy and vitality
- Improves circulation and heart health
- Associated with blood purification
- Aids in the absorption of vitamins and minerals

2. Emotional healing:
- Considered a stone of passion and commitment
- Promotes self-confidence and courage
- Alleviates emotional disharmony
- Stimulate feelings of joy and hope

3. Mental healing:
- Enhances mental clarity and focus
- Stimulates creativity and imagination
- Boosts willpower and motivation
- Helps overcome crisis or trauma

4. Spiritual healing:
- Considered a stone of spiritual fire and transformation
- Associated with grounding
- Thought to enhance one's spiritual awareness

STONE: LAPIS LAZULI | SAPPIR

Tribe: Dan

Frequency Range: 294-301 Hz

Hebrew writing: סַפִּיר

ס (Samech) - Represents divine support and circular motion. As the first letter it creates a protective circle of light around the stone's energy field. This relates to lapis lazuli's protective and supportive properties, particularly in spiritual communication.

פּ (Peh with dagesh) - The emphasised Peh represents powerful speech and divine utterance. The dagesh (dot) intensifies this property.

י (Yod) - The divine spark of creation represents the highest wisdom. In lapis, it facilitates connection to cosmic consciousness and primordial wisdom.

ר (Resh) - Represents the head/cosmic consciousness. As the final letter it completes the circuit by bringing the stone's energy to resonate with Christ's higher thinking - facilitating the mind of Christ to be expanded in our awareness and consciousness.

Together, these letters create a sophisticated spiritual communication circuit: Samech initiates a protective field of support, emphasised Peh activates clear communication, Yod connects to the Spirit of Wisdom and Resh completes the circuit in higher consciousness. The vowel points create important modulations: Patach opens channels of reception and Chirik helps penetrate spiritual mysteries.

This letter combination explains lapis lazuli's traditional properties:
- Enhancement of spiritual communication
- Access to ancient wisdom and records
- Connection to cosmic consciousness

The letter structure explains lapis lazuli's reputation as a stone of royalty and spiritual communication - the letters create a complete circuit from divine protection (Samech) through clear speech (Peh) to cosmic consciousness (Resh), with Yod providing the divine spark that activates the entire system.

PHYSICAL PROPERTIES

1. Physical healing:
- Alleviates throat and vocal cord issues
- Boosts the immune system
- Reduces inflammation
- Helps with migraines and headaches

2. Emotional healing:
- Considered a stone of truth and friendship
- Promotes self-awareness and self-expression
- Alleviates stress and brings emotional balance
- Enhances confidence and self-esteem

3. Mental healing:
- Enhances intellectual ability and memory
- Simulates the desire for knowledge and truth
- Enhances problem-solving skills
- Promotes clarity and objectivity in thinking

4. Spiritual healing:
- Considered a stone of wisdom and spiritual enlightenment
- Associated with expanding awareness and spiritual vision
- Thought to facilitate spiritual journeys and dream work
- Thought to enhance creativity and intuition

STONE: WHITE ONYX | SHOHAM

Tribe: Naphtali

Frequency Range: 7,500 - 8,000 Hz

Hebrew writing: שֹׁהַם

שׁ (Shin) - Represents divine fire and transformation. In white onyx, it acts as a purifying force helping to transmute and cleanse energies. The three prongs of Shin represent the three columns of manifestation - intention, resonance and creation.

ה (Hey) - Represents the breath of Yahweh and revelation. It works with the stone's ability to reveal hidden truths, destroy distorted perspectives and facilitate spiritual understanding. Hey also represents Holy Spirit, Yahweh's divine feminine and maternal presence.

ם (Mem Sofit) - The final form of Mem represents the waters of creation and completion. As the closing letter it contains and circulates the purified energies within the stone's matrix.

These letters create a purification and transformation circuit: Shin initiates divine fire purification, Hey brings divine breath and revelation and final Mem contains and stabilises the purified energies. The vowel points serve crucial functions: Cholam elevates the purifying frequency and Patach opens channels for healing.

This letter combination explains white onyx's traditional properties:
- Purification and cleansing
- Grounding and stabilising
- Enhancement of intuition
- Balance of duality

The letter structure explains white onyx's reputation as a stone of purification and protection - the letters create a perfect circuit that begins with divine fire (Shin), moves through revelation (Hey) and is contained in the waters of creation (Mem Sofit).

The combination of fire (Shin) and water (Mem) elements in the name creates a powerful alchemical process within the stone, emphasising its ability to both transform and stabilise energies. The Hey placed between them acts as a bridge between these opposing forces, allowing for perfect balance.

PHYSICAL PROPERTIES

1. Physical healing:
- Strengthens the immune system
- Aids in healing bone marrow and teeth

- Associated with improving skin disorders
- Helps regulate water retention in the body

2. Emotional healing:
- Considered a stone of inner strength and self-control
- Helps manage stress and anxiety
- Promotes emotional stability
- Aids in overcoming negative emotions like grief or fear

3. Mental healing:
- Enhances focus and concentration
- Improves logical thinking and decision-making
- Boosts memory and learning abilities
- Promotes mental discipline and willpower

4. Spiritual healing:
- Considered a stone of protection and grounding
- Associated with enhancing intuition and inner wisdom
- Thought to facilitate meditation and spiritual growth

STONE: AMBER | CHASHMAL

Tribe: Gad

Frequency Range: 5,000 - 8,000 Hz

Hebrew writing: חַשְׁמַל

ח (Chet) - Represents life force and a barrier/fence. As the first letter, it creates a protective field that contains amber's powerful electrical properties. Chet also represents the fusion of energies in relation to amber's formation from tree resin.

שׁ (Shin) - Represents divine fire and transformation. In amber, it works with the stone's solar properties and its ability to generate electromagnetic energy when rubbed. The three prongs of Shin represent the threefold nature of energy transmission.

מ (Mem) - Symbolises water and the womb of creation. In amber it represents the fluid, adaptable nature of the stone's energy and its connection to ancient life forces.

ל (Lamed) - The tallest letter in the Hebrew alphabet represents teaching and direction of energy. As the final letter, it guides amber's energy upward while maintaining a sense of being grounded.

Together, these letters create a sophisticated electromagnetic circuit: Chet contains and protects the energy field, Shin activates electromagnetic properties, Mem provides fluidity and life force and Lamed directs and teaches through the energy. The vowel points play important roles: multiple Patach points create flowing channels and Shva balances the intense energies.

This letter combination explains amber's traditional properties:
- Electromagnetic energy generation
- Ancient wisdom preservation
- Energy protection and transmutation
- Teaching and knowledge transfer

The configuration reveals why amber is particularly effective for:
- Energy cleansing (Chet's protective field)
- Electromagnetic healing (Shin's fire properties)
- Ancient memory access (Mem's primordial waters)
- Spiritual teaching (Lamed's guidance)

Interestingly, חַשְׁמַל (Amber) also means "electricity" in modern Hebrew, showing the direct connection between the living letters and amber's electrical properties. This name reveals amber's role as a bridge between ancient organic wisdom (fossilised resin) and electromagnetic energy (its triboelectric properties - the process by which two uncharged objects become electrically charged when they come into contact and then separate.).

PHYSICAL PROPERTIES

1. Physical healing:
- Boosts the immune system
- Alleviates pain, especially in joints
- Detoxifies the body
- Helps with thyroid issues and hormone balance

2. Emotional healing:
- Considered a stone of positivity and warmth
- Alleviates depression and anxiety
- Promotes emotional balance and stability
- Said to help overcome fears and phobias

3. Mental healing:
- Enhances memory and decision-making
- Stimulates intellect and creativity
- Promotes mental clarity and focus
- Helps with overcoming mental blocks

4. Spiritual healing:
- Believed to cleanse the energy field around you
- Thought to promote patience and wisdom

STONE: AGATE | SHEVO

Tribe: Asher

Frequency Range: 4,000 - 6,500 Hz

Hebrew writing: שְׁבוֹ

שׁ (Shin) - Shin represents divine fire and transformation. In agate, it acts as the primary processor of earthly energies, helping to transmute and organise them into banded patterns (reflecting agate's physical structure). The three prongs of Shin represent the three levels of reality that agate bridges: physical, emotional and spiritual.

ב (Bet) - Represents house/container. In agate, it works with the stone's ability to create protected space and contain healing energies. It especially relates to how agate's bands create multiple "houses" or chambers of energy.

וֹ (Vav with Cholam) - Vav represents the connector/hook between heaven and earth, while the Cholam vowel point above represents elevation. Together they create a channel for divine energy to flow through the stone's layered structure.

Together, these letters create a sophisticated grounding and protection circuit: Shin initiates energy transformation, Bet creates safe containment spaces, Vav channels and directs the energies and the vowel points moderate the flow.

This letter combination explains agate's traditional properties:
- Grounding and stabilisation
- Protection and security
- Harmonious energy flow
- Pattern organisation
- Emotional balance

The configuration shows why agate is particularly effective for:
- Energy organisation (Shin's transformative power)
- Creating safe space (Bet's containing force)
- Connecting different energy levels (Vav's bridging ability)
- Stabilizing emotions (Shva's balancing effect)

The letter structure explains agate's reputation as a stone of stabilisation and harmonious arrangement. The letters create a perfect circuit that transforms energy (Shin), contains it (Bet), and then channels it appropriately (Vav). The arrangement mirrors agate's physical banding, where each layer serves a specific purpose in the overall energetic structure.

The combination particularly supports agate's ability to create ordered patterns from chaos (Shin-Bet interaction) and grounding spiritual energy into physical form (Vav's connecting power) while maintaining emotional stability (balanced vowel points).

PHYSICAL PROPERTIES

1. Physical healing:
   - Improves digestion and relieve gastritis
   - Enhances the function of the lymphatic system
   - Strengthens the eyes and heals skin disorders
   - Aids in treating insomnia and promote restful sleep

2. Emotional healing:
   - Considered a stabilising and strengthening stone
   - Calms and soothes emotional distress
   - Promotes inner peace and self-acceptance
   - Helps overcome negativity and bitterness

3. Mental healing:
   - Enhances mental function and improves concentration
   - Promotes analytical capabilities and perceptiveness
   - Enhances memory and stimulates thinking
   - Helps balance the left and right brain hemispheres

4. Spiritual healing:
   - Considered a grounding stone that promotes stability
   - Believed to enhance spiritual growth and inner awareness

STONE: AMETHYST | ACHLAMAH

Tribe: Issachar

Frequency Range: 400-900 Hz

Hebrew writing: אַחְלָמָה

א (Aleph) - The first letter represents unity and divine creative force. In amethyst it channels pure spiritual light and transformation. As the first letter of the alphabet, it connects to amethyst's ability to initiate spiritual awakening.

ח (Chet) - Represents life force and divine protection. In amethyst it works with the stone's protective and purifying qualities, especially against negative energies and addictive patterns.

ל (Lamed) - The tallest letter, represents teaching and direction. It facilitates amethyst's role in spiritual instruction and elevation of consciousness.

מ (Mem) - Represents water and the womb of creation, working with amethyst's flowing spiritual energies and intuitive wisdom.

ה (Hey) - The final letter represents Yahweh's breath and revelation. It completes the circuit by bringing divine presence into manifestation.

Together, these letters create a powerful spiritual transformation circuit: Aleph initiates divine light transmission, Chet provides protection during transformation, Lamed guides the spiritual teaching process, Mem flows with intuitive wisdom and Hey brings divine revelation. The vowel points create crucial modulations: Patach opens spiritual channels, Shva balances high frequencies and the double Kamatz creates fullness of experience.

This letter combination explains amethyst's traditional properties:
- Spiritual awakening and transformation
- Protection from negative energies
- Enhancement of intuition and wisdom
- Sobriety and clarity of mind
- Connection to divine guidance

The letter structure explains amethyst's reputation as a stone of spiritual sobriety and transformation - the letters create a complete circuit from divine light (Aleph) through protection (Chet) and teaching (Lamed) to final revelation (Hey).

The sequence particularly supports:
- Transformation of lower energies to higher frequencies
- Protection during spiritual work
- Clear connection to divine guidance
- Integration of spiritual wisdom

PHYSICAL PROPERTIES

1. Physical healing:
- Enhances the immune system

- Reduces headaches and migraines
- Improves sleep quality
- Aids in detoxification and reducing addictive behaviours

2. Emotional healing:
- Considered a stone of peace and tranquility
- Alleviates stress and anxiety
- Balances mood swings
- Promotes emotional centring and contentment

3. Mental healing:
- Enhances mental clarity and focus
- Improves memory and motivation
- Boosts creativity and imagination
- Aids in decision-making and problem-solving

4. Spiritual healing:
- Believed to enhance intuition
- Associated with deepening meditation practices

STONE: BERYL | YAHALOM

Tribe: Zebulun

Frequency Range: 7,000 - 9,000 Hz

Hebrew writing: יָהֲלֹם

י (Yod) - The smallest letter, represents the divine spark and point of creation. In beryl, it initiates the stone's ability to focus and concentrate light and spiritual energy. As the first letter, it connects to beryl's precision and clarity.

ה (Hey) - Represents Yahweh's breath and revelation. It works with the stone's ability to reveal truth and bring illumination. Hey also represents the feminine presence of Ruach (Holy Spirit) and the maternal qualities of Yahweh.

ל (Lamed) - The tallest letter represents teaching and direction. It works with beryl's ability to direct and focus energy upward while maintaining a sense of being grounded.

מ (Mem Sofit) - The final form of Mem represents the waters of completion. As the closing letter, it contains and circulates the focused energies within beryl's crystal structure.

Together, these letters create a sophisticated light-focusing circuit: Yod initiates precise divine spark, Hey brings illumination, Lamed directs energy upward and final Mem contains and circulates. The vowel points serve crucial functions: Kamatz creates fullness of energy, Chataf Patach enables swift transformation and Cholam elevates consciousness.

This letter combination explains beryl's traditional properties:
- Focus and clarity
- Light amplification
- Truth revelation
- Energy direction
- Spiritual insight

The configuration shows why beryl is particularly effective for:
- Concentration (Yod's focused point)
- Illumination (Hey's revealing light)
- Spiritual guidance (Lamed's direction)
- Energy containment (Mem Sofit's completing waters)

The letter structure explains beryl's reputation as a stone of focus and illumination - the letters create a perfect circuit that begins with precise divine spark (Yod), moves through revelation (Hey), is directed upward (Lamed) and is contained in completion (Mem Sofit).

PHYSICAL PROPERTIES

1. Physical healing:
- Strengthens the circulatory system
- Aids in treating disorders of the spine and bones

- Improves eye health
- Enhances the body's detoxification processes

2. Emotional healing:
- Considered a stone of courage and confidence
- Reduces stress and promotes calmness
- Enhance happiness and joviality
- Strengthen relationships and promote fidelity

3. Mental healing:
- Enhance mental clarity and sharpness
- Improves concentration and learning abilities
- Stimulates creativity and imagination
- Aids in overcoming mental fatigue

4. Spiritual healing:
- Thought to facilitate communication with Wisdom

STONE: SARDONYX | SOHAM

Tribe: Joseph

Frequency Range: 7,000 - 8,500 Hz

Hebrew writing: יָשְׁפֵה

י (Yod) - Represents the divine spark and primordial point of manifestation. In sardonyx, it acts as the initiator of grounding divine will into matter, particularly relating to the stone's banded structure's ability to organise energy.

שׁ (Shin) - Represents divine fire and transformation. It works with the stone's ability to transform and align energies through its layered structure.

פ (Peh) - Symbolises the mouth/speech and manifestation. In sardonyx, it works with the stone's ability to help manifest divine will and speak truth with authority.

ה (Hey) - The final letter represents Yahweh's breath and revelation. It completes the circuit by bringing divine presence into physical manifestation through the stone's structure.

Together, these letters create a sophisticated grounding and manifestation circuit: Yod initiates divine will, Shin transforms energies through layers, Peh manifests through speech/action and Hey brings final revelation. The vowel points serve the following functions: Patach opens channels for flow, Shva balances between layers and Tzere directs manifestation.

This letter combination explains sardonyx's traditional properties:
- Grounding spiritual energy
- Protection and stability
- Enhanced willpower
- Clear communication
- Manifestation of primordial purpose

The configuration shows why sardonyx is particularly effective for:
- Organising energy (layered structure reflected in letters)
- Speaking truth with authority (Peh's oral powers)
- Maintaining focus (Tzere's directing force)
- Grounding spiritual insight (Hey's manifestation)

This letter structure explains sardonyx's reputation as a stone of grounded protection and purposeful manifestation - the letters create a perfect circuit from divine spark (Yod) through transformation (Shin) to manifestation (Peh) and revelation (Hey).

PHYSICAL PROPERTIES

1. Physical healing:
   - Enhance stamina and vigour
   - Supports bone health and the immune system
   - Improves coordination and balance
   - Aids in regulating body fluids

2. Emotional healing:
- Considered a stone of strength and protection
- Promotes willpower and self-control
- Enhances emotional stability
- Boosts confidence and assertiveness

3. Mental healing:
- Enhances focus and discipline
- Improves logical thinking and rationality
- Aids in clear communication
- Promotes integrity and virtuous conduct

4. Spiritual healing:
- Considered a grounding and stabilising stone
- Believed to bring spiritual strength during times of strife
- Thought to enhance one's connection to the earth

STONE: JASPER | YASHPEH

Tribe: Benjamin

Frequency Range: 5,000 - 7,000 Hz

Hebrew writing: יָשְׁפֵה

יּ (Yod) - As the first letter, represents the divine spark but in jasper specifically works with earth element initiation. It seeds the primordial patterns into matter, particularly connecting to jasper's ability to ground and structure earth energies.

שׁ (Shin) - Represents divine fire, but in jasper it manifests as the warming, nurturing aspect of earth's energy. Its three prongs represent the three aspects of jasper's earth connection: grounding, nurturing and protecting.

פ (Peh) - In jasper specifically, represents the mouth of creation and the primordial wisdom being communicated. Works with the stone's ability to facilitate ancient wisdom and earth's memories or record.

ה (Hey) - The final letter brings Yahwe's divine breath into matter. In jasper, it specifically works with how the stone breathes with the earth's rhythms and cycles.

Together, these letters create an earth-wisdom circuit: Yod plants divine patterns into earth, Shin warms and activates earth energies, Peh speaks earth wisdom and Hey breathes life into earthly forms. The vowel points serve the following functions: Kamatz completes earth connection, Shva stabilises in material realm and Tzere focuses earth energies

This letter combination explains jasper's traditional properties:
- Deep earth connection
- Stability and grounding
- Access to land's memories
- Manifestation through natural law

The configuration shows why jasper is particularly effective for:
- Earth healing and integration with earth rhythms (Yod-Shin interaction)
- Communication with nature (Peh's speaking)
- Maintaining stability (Shva's grounding force)
- Connecting to the Spirit of Wisdom (Hey's living breath)

This letter structure explains jasper's reputation as supreme grounding stone - creating a circuit from heaven to earth that maintains perfect stability while allowing access to wisdom.

PHYSICAL PROPERTIES

1. Physical healing:
- Supports the digestive system

- Strengthens the liver and gallbladder
- Aids in detoxification of the body
- Aids in regulating mineral balance

2. Emotional healing:
- Considered a nurturing and protective stone
- Promotes feelings of wholeness and tranquility
- Alleviates stress and anxiety
- Facilitates feelings of comfort and security

3. Mental healing:
- Enhances mental endurance
- Promotes organisational abilities
- Aids in problem-solving and quick thinking
- Stimulates imagination and creativity

4. Spiritual healing:
- Considered a grounding and stabilising stone

CHAPTER 10
A Guide to Cleansing Gemstones

Cleansing gemstones and crystals is an important practice for restoring their natural energetic state and enhancing their metaphysical properties. By regularly cleansing these powerful stones, you can ensure they are operating at their full potential and are able to provide the desired spiritual, emotional and energetic benefits.

There are several effective methods for cleansing gemstones and crystals:

1. Sunlight

Placing your stones in direct sunlight for a few hours is a simple yet potent cleansing technique. The sun's radiant energy helps to clear away any negative or stagnant vibrations the stones may have absorbed. This method is particularly useful for quartz, citrine and other stones that thrive in solar energy. However, it's important to exercise caution with stones like amethyst, which can fade in strong sunlight.

2. Sound and Prayer

Exposing your gemstones and crystals to harmonious sounds can also be an effective cleansing method. Using your own voice through chanting, singing or affirmations, or playing soothing frequency music, singing bowls, bells or tuning forks near the stones can help to clear and recharge their energy. Additionally, you can incorporate prayers, mantras or other spiritual practices during the sound cleansing process to further amplify the effects.

3. Salt Water

Submerging your stones in a bowl of pure, natural salt water is an effective way to cleanse and purify them. The salt helps to draw out any negative or stagnant energies while the water provides a gentle, nurturing medium for the cleansing process. This method is suitable for most gemstones but caution should be taken with porous stones or those containing metal, as the salt water may cause damage.

4. Breath

Your breath carries the same magnificent frequency as that of Yahweh, since it is His breath blown into man that gives life.

Greg Ordway, a wonderful son of God and dear friend, has a unique understanding as well as profound relationship with the 22 living letters, and he pointed out to me that 'Eben' (Hebrew for 'stone') has a numerical value of 53, which is 'Hey' meaning breath and 'Gimmel' meaning provision. If you should add your breath to this equation, which means adding another 5 (Hey) you will get to 58. 58 is the Hebrew word 'Nogah' and means 'brilliancy or bright light'.

> "So we, as most loved of Yahweh, can put our breath into a stone and release the brilliance that Yahweh put into it allowing the bright light or frequency to shine/radiate out of it." - Greg Ordway

This is a beautiful way to engage with stones and bring their frequency into resonance with the eternal breath of life - cleansing, restoring and charging the stone with Yeshua's eternal light.

Regularly incorporating these various cleansing methods into your gemstone and crystal care routine will ensure that your stones remain vibrant, potent and aligned with your spiritual and energetic needs. When properly cleansed, these stones can interact more effectively with your body's natural energy field, helping to bring your frequency into a more coherent state. Many practitioners report feeling increased vitality, mental clarity and emotional balance when working with freshly cleansed stones.

Cleansed crystals can be particularly powerful when placed directly on the body during meditation or healing practices. For example, a purified rose quartz may help open the heart energy field, promoting the release of trauma and heartache, while a cleansed amethyst can facilitate the release of anxiety, depressions and addictive tendencies. Some users find that sleeping with cleansed stones under their pillow helps promote restful sleep and vivid dreams.

Cleansing Method	Stones
Sunlight	All except Amethyst and Beryl
Sound and Prayer	All stones
Salt Water	All except Amber
Breath	All stones

A WORD FROM THE AUTHOR

Since childhood, I've dreamt of writing a book. This work, the first to flow from my pen, has been an incredible journey of revelation and growth guided by the Holy Spirit.

My deepest hope and prayer for you, dear reader, is that through these pages, you'll discover the majesty and beauty of Yahweh in a fresh, awe-inspiring way. May His glorious light, divine sound and heavenly atmosphere become the axis around which your life revolves.

As you delve into the spiritual technologies explored in this book, I pray you'll experience the richness of Yeshua's favour. May this adventure equip and transform you, drawing you ever closer to the heart of our Creator.

Thank you for joining me on this exploration. May your journey through these pages be blessed and enlightening.

Blessings

Bianca van Staden

ABOUT THE AUTHOR

Bianca van Staden, founder of Oak Ministries, lives in South Africa with her husband, Scharl van Staden, where together they run Wells of Mem Christ-centred Mystic Church. She specialises in Deep Emotional Therapy and Wellness and Prayer Coaching. She desires to see the sons of God walk in holistic health and see the earth liberated and whole, restored to its original intent as the garden of Yahweh's pleasure. She is passionate about exploring the deep mysteries of Christ and believe the sons of God have unclaimed inheritances and has devoted herself to help believers access and embrace these treasures.

If you are interested in exploring Bianca's coaching services, she offers online sessions tailored to individual needs. To connect with Bianca or book a session, you can contact her at oakministriessa@gmail.com or reach out on Facebook or Instagram.

OAK MINISTRIES
Life & Wellness Coaching | Trauma & Stress Resilience Coaching

Welcome to your journey towards a more fulfilling and empowered life

My goal is to equip you with skills to navigate through life's challenges & unlock your full potential. Tailored coaching sessions are aimed to empower your strengths, facilitate inner- & trauma healing & build resilience.

Coaching Services Offered:
- Personal Development
- Wellness & Health
- Career & Productivity
- Relationships
- Mindset & Stress Management
- Spiritual & Prayer Coaching
- Trauma & Inner Healing

BIANCA VAN STADEN | FOUNDER
DEEP EMOTIONAL THERAPIST
PRAYER COACH

SeraphCreative
Heaven's Heart for Earth

Seraph Creative is a collective of artists, writers, theologians & illustrators who desire to see the body of Christ grow into full maturity, walking in their inheritance as Sons Of God on the Earth.

Sign up to our newsletter to know about other exciting releases.

Visit our website:
www.seraphcreative.org

Made in United States
North Haven, CT
09 April 2025